HOUSES OF STUDY

Houses of Study

A Jewish Woman among Books

ILANA M. BLUMBERG

University of Nebraska Press | Lincoln and London

Library of Congress Cataloging-in-Publication Data
Blumberg, Ilana M., 1970–
Houses of study : a Jewish woman among books /
Ilana M. Blumberg.
p. cm.
ISBN-13: 978-0-8032-1367-8 (cloth : alk. paper)
ISBN-10: 0-8032-1367-0 (cloth : alk. paper)
1. Blumberg, Ilana M., 1970– 2. Jews—Michigan—
Ann Arbor—Biography. 3. Blumberg, Ilana M., 1970–
 —Books and reading. 4. Blumberg, Ilana M., 1970–
 —Religion. 5. Ann Arbor (Mich.)—Biography.
I. Title.
F558.2.J5B58 2007
305.892′4077435—dc22
[B]   2006020756

Set in Scala by Keystone Typesetting, Inc.
Designed by A. Shahan.

For my parents

GENESIS 15:17. **"And it was blackness"**: It was not like the darkness of night in which you can still see your way to walk. But [Abraham] saw that it was like the blackness of those who sit in an enclosed place into which no ray of light can enter, in which they can but grope [to find their way]. Such would be the travels of his descendants among the nations. And he saw further.

"And behold, a smoking furnace and a torch of fire": From the force of persecutions, the light of deliverance appears suddenly. . . . It is not as if you see who has kindled the light, but instead, from a whirling smoke column, comes suddenly, light! Similarly, the process of deliverance under God's direction will be so hidden that it will be impossible to see how there might ever be light. But the light is the covenant.

RABBI NAFTALI TZVI YEHUDAH BERLIN (1817–1893),
Ha'amek Davar

The rain had ceased, and the light from the breaking clouds fell on Savonarola as he left the Loggia in the midst of his guard, walking as he had come, with the Sacrament in his hand. But there seemed no glory in the light that fell on him now, no smile of heaven: it was only that light which shines on, patiently and impartially, justifying or condemning by simply showing all things in the slow history of their ripening.

GEORGE ELIOT, *Romola,* chapter 65 (1863)

Contents

Preface

When I was a child in the 1970s, I always imagined that I went to school twice as long as the other children on my block. By the time I was a teenager, my school day extended from eight in the morning until five-thirty in the afternoon. In the harsh Chicago winters, I arrived in the dark and left in the dark.

Living in school, as my friends and I did, made a strange kind of sense because our private school was meant to educate us for life. In the morning, we prayed and spoke in Hebrew as we studied Torah, Mishnah, Midrash, Jewish law, and history. In the afternoon and into the early evening, we spoke English as we studied math, science, literature, and world history. This was our "double curriculum," the fare of Jewish day school students across the United States. And the hope of parents and teachers: that a traditionally educated American Jewish child would come to see that she could live in both worlds—Jewish and secular—happily, healthily, without (much) compromise.

Yet as I turned sixteen or so and our daily household mail delivery became heavy with college brochures and applications, I recognized that the ever-extending school day, seemingly capacious enough for all things, would reach its limits. Parents and teachers could decide to extend school by an hour or even two but not by years, decades, or a lifetime. Soon we would leave home. Our training as young Jews, in home and school, would come to its end, and we would no longer come and go constrained, gifted by the demands and abundances of the "double curriculum." Then the true test of our childhood educations would arrive as we left home to live in that world for which we had been doubly prepared—that world with paradoxically fewer divisions but many more choices.

No one thought our educations would be complete at age eighteen. Both my parents had gone to yeshiva day school in the 1950s and then college and graduate school in the 1960s and 1970s; both my paternal grandparents had completed graduate degrees by the end of the first third of the twentieth century. Over two generations, my family had found itself in universities from New York to Boston to Michigan: CCNY, NYU, the Jewish Theological Seminary, and Columbia; BU, MIT, and Harvard; the University of Michigan, Eastern Michigan. Clearly I too would go to college. I hoped to study literature.

As graduation from yeshiva high school grew nearer, questions arose: for those of us who planned to attend a secular institution rather than a Jewish university such as Yeshiva University or Stern College for Women, how would we continue to build from both sides? Had all our mornings devoted to Hebrew, Torah, and Jewish thought and law been spent without a future of learning in mind? Was Jewish learning just a practice of childhood, to be left behind when one "grew up"?

In the late 1980s (as still today) common practice provided an answer. We, Orthodox high school graduates, boys and girls both, were encouraged to spend a year of study in intensive, single-sex yeshivas in Israel before returning to America to attend university. In these yeshivas Jewish texts would be both bread and water of life. In these houses of study there would be no afternoon periods of math, science, literature, or social studies. Instead, there would be Torah in all its many manifestations, in the widest sense of the term: Jewish learning from the span of centuries, a rich spectrum of rabbinic voices, morning to night, Sabbath to Sabbath, every season of the year. This school would never end.

When our parents and teachers evoked this world for us, in most cases it was not because they envisioned it as sufficient for a lifetime—not our lifetimes in any case. The men and women who taught in such yeshivas, who lived in Israel, had made choices other than the ones we were to make. Most of them had never and would never spend four years at Columbia University or the University of Pennsylvania. Many had university degrees, but it was always remarkable, always worth mentioning, when those degrees came from secular institutions and were granted in fields thoroughly distinct from Jewish study. As I imagined it, we were to be one-year guests in other people's real lives, as though we were jumping on and off a merry-go-round that never stopped, ascending and alighting while it continued to move.

My parents left in my hands the choice to study in Israel, as they left to me the selection of university. But granting me this autonomy was not typical for our community and suggested that my parents were not wholly integrated members of the adult pack. And in truth my parents were distinct from others by virtue of having raised and schooled us—me, my brother, and my sister—in not only Orthodox schools and synagogues, but also in institutions belonging to the more liberal Conservative Jewish movement. Summer camp, elementary school, and my early life in synagogue were all lived among Conservative Jews.

While my parents were not typical Orthodox Jews, they were not typical Conservative Jews either. They themselves had grown up in Orthodox synagogues (a synagogue *meant* Orthodox in the 1940s and 1950s), Orthodox summer camps, and yeshiva day schools. They had attained fluency in modern Hebrew and classical Judaic texts. My siblings and I were consequently second-generation literate Jews, while most of my friends in Conservative schools were the first generations in their families to speak, read, write, study, sing, and pray conversantly in Hebrew.

I do not know precisely why my parents chose to move left into Conservative Judaism for the period of my childhood and early adolescence. I do know that both my mother and father grew up in second-generation American families whose practice had veered away from the strictures observed by the previous immigrant generation so that the educations my parents received at home and at school were not wholly aligned. I know also that my parents became adults in major American cities and college towns in the late 1960s, not sites or an era known for fostering a commitment to traditional styles of living.

Today it seems to me that what Conservative Judaism had to recommend itself to young American parents in the 1970s was its egalitarianism. Where Orthodox institutions were dominantly structured by divisions of sex, Conservative Jewish leaders and rabbis were following more closely and more quickly the pulse of American life. The 1970s mania to give trucks to girls and dolls to boys—and all the serious implications of the women's movement and the sexual revolution—challenged religious establishments to offer their adherents a way of educating children that would reflect a basic belief that boys and girls had equal and shared opportunities. In practice what this meant for me as a young girl in Conservative settings was that my brother and I could both stand before the congregation to lead it in the hymn that closed the Sabbath services. When we visited my mother's parents' Orthodox synagogue, I sat next to my mother and grandmother and leaned over the rim of the high balcony, watching the tiny men below as the Torah passed through their aisles but not ours.

Though my elementary education was in Conservative Jewish day schools, by the time I reached high school, my parents found themselves without choices to make *among* schools. In all Chicago there was no Conservative Jewish high school. If they wanted us in Jewish schools, the schools would have to be Orthodox. Like that of their parents before them, my parents' commitment to Jewish education ran deep and strong. It would never have occurred to them to allow me or my siblings to skip high school, to send us out into the world at fourteen to seek our fortunes. Why, then, would it be reasonable to assume that our Jewish educations were sufficient for life at age fourteen?

When I began to study in an Orthodox high school, my family's practice returned to the Orthodoxy neither branch of it had known comprehensively in three generations. But it was not an extreme "return," like that of the penitent *Baal T'shu-vah* movement. It was a return that retained the cadences of childhood, of girlhood. It was a return in which I remembered standing on the *bimah* (raised platform) with my brother, singing and looking out at a congregation undivided by sex. It was a return that begged questions that motivate my writing here.

The Modern Orthodox school I attended took as its password, as its holy aim, "Torah U'Madda," the remarkable synthesis of Jewish learning and Western secular knowledge garnered from ancient times to modern. No wonder we were in school from morning to night.

What "Torah U'Madda" meant beyond the life of study was that a good Jew lived in the world, eyes open. A good Jewish life would be best shaped not only by the teachings of Torah, but also by the most valuable wisdom of non-Jews. Though this may sound unremarkable and unobjectionable, one did not have to look far to find those who objected and rejected vehemently. Ultra-Orthodox or Haredi Jews (the sort of antique Jews that many Americans imagine when they hear the term "Orthodox") were recognizable and distinct from Modern Orthodox Jews by virtue of their rejection of modernity: their eighteenth-century garb, their black hats and long coats, the men with long beards and the boys with curly *payes,* or sidelocks; the tones of Yiddish in the stores, synagogues, and streets; the ritualized early marriages, often arranged; the abundance of modestly dressed and wigged young mothers and grandmothers; the short spans between generations working to safeguard against change.

Modern Orthodox as well as Conservative Jews rejected the rejectionism just as vociferously as the ultra-Orthodox scorned the blending or reconciliation of cultures. We Moderns prided ourselves on being able to "negotiate" the divides and the overlaps. "Tradition and modernity" was a phrase that rang in my ears in the years from fourteen to twenty-four.

As proud as the bearers of the "Torah U'Madda" slogan were, as the time approached for parents who had come of age in the 1960s to send their children off, not a few wondered if perhaps those ultra-Orthodox Jews who would not touch the fires of university with a ten-foot pole knew something after all. Could anything assure a child's commitment to the past and his or her cognate commitment to the future in the absence of parents? Even those parents sending their children to Orthodox institutions knew that New York City lay right beyond the door.

Ostensibly the idea of studying in Israel before moving on to university was merely an extrapolation of the "Torah U'Madda" approach that made Torah a morning activity and Madda an afternoon one. Our time frame would be years now rather than days; our map would be countries rather than classrooms. But the combination suddenly carried a different charge. When our teachers and rabbis and some of our parents pressed us toward Torah study in Israel, they spoke of it as though it were its own good. But underneath that thought hovered the adult consideration, half spoken, half secret: perhaps a year of intensive Jewish study might succeed in blunting the future temptations and dangers of unadulterated secularity, the pleasures and risks that awaited us on American college campuses.

In dividing up what had seemed whole—Torah (in Israel), then *Madda* (in America)—our parents and teachers and rabbis acknowledged in practice what they had never precisely said aloud: the reconciliation of modernity and tradition was actually rather difficult and required what my bubbi (grandmother) would have called some "finagling" or crafty maneuvering. The key of anxiety alerted me to this as much as anything else.

What I would come quickly to discover as I moved from adolescence to adulthood was that traditional and secular ideas often posed serious problems for each other. At times it seemed they simply could not be sustained jointly. What you read in Aristotle or Faulkner what you absorbed of evolutionary biology or cosmogony threatened to split away—and perhaps to split you away—from the path of Torah. The modern values of self-expression and realization—"finding yourself"—would not always be compatible with Jewish teachings and strictures. And those personal, internal crises, forceful and frightening as they were, did not even skirt such public, political issues as abortion or homosexuality and what the appropriate response of contemporary religion might be.

By the time I began my university studies, I could see that the chief pattern of my childhood—the morning-afternoon divide between what we had called "Limudei Kodesh," Holy Learning, and the banal, descriptionless "General Studies"—would no longer effectively be soldered by lunch and recess. The changing of the guard, when our Jewishly learned teachers left school and our "generally" learned teachers arrived, had not been an overlap but a thorough, gaping fissure. Perhaps I would not have come to see this so arrestingly and so quickly had I not been born a girl.

The story I tell in the pages to come begins in 1988, when I landed in Israel, eighteen years old and female. My cross-cultural education began with a lesson in language. The term "yeshiva" (seminary), I quickly learned, did not apply to girls or women. In America, our teachers had talked about our year of study in "yeshiva" without distinguishing between male and female students and institutions. But when I got to Israel, conversations in Hebrew came to a standstill when Jews, both religious and secular, asked me why I'd come to Israel and I explained that I'd come to learn in "yeshiva." I'd used the wrong term, they explained. Girls and young women went to *mikhlala* (women's college), not *yeshiva*.

It was what we might call a semantic difference; it didn't change what I'd come to do. But the existence of two terms for what I'd thought was one separate but equal endeavor alerted me to a new doubleness. This was not a division between "Torah U'Madda" but between men and women. *Mikhlala* conjured images of young women of marriageable age sitting in rows of desks, an extension of high school, with a married religious woman teaching them material in what Americans would call a mode of "frontal education," the transmission of knowledge from the teacher's side of the desk to the student's. *Yeshiva* conjured rooms filled with long tables, men of all ages sitting on either sides of the tables, studying with each other, reading the Talmud aloud, debating its meanings, engaging in a lifetime practice that could be sustained without a teacher, though independent study alternated with *shiur*, rabbinic lessons about the material prepared. These were stereotypes to be sure, and stereotypes that would come to be violated regularly by girls, women, and *mikhlalot* (women's colleges) in the years that followed. Nonetheless, when I arrived at Barnard College twelve months later, no one told me that "college" was not the term I was looking for.

Nearly twenty years have passed since I left my childhood family and home and made my first forays into the Beit Midrash and the university, the two "houses of study" I would inhabit independently as an adult. But any adult resolution I have achieved between these two worlds still yields frequently to my sense of deep conflict. For more than ten years conflict was so dominantly my experience that I assumed adulthood *meant* the force that pulled things apart.

There were two languages and literatures that I spoke and read, that I meant to keep speaking and reading. Quite literally my books were divided between two bookcases: Torah, which went from right to left, its titles in Hebrew and Aramaic, a rich collection of classical Judaic texts; and *Madda,* which went from left to right, its titles in English, an unending cascade of novels, essays, poetry, and drama spanning the fourteenth through twentieth centuries. But these two literatures could not easily be had in the same country, let alone the same school. They could not be taught by the same people (then why did we assume they could be *learned* by the same people?), and they could not address the same questions in the same fashion.

Just as bodies of knowledge were divided when a child became an adult, so too sex suddenly mattered as it never had before. A Jewish woman could not elude her body, could not slip out of it as the Jewish girl could. My body, suddenly meaningful, was also indivisible. I could be in only one place at one time, within one community, not another.

In the years of early adulthood, I clung to the single ideal unquestionably shared by Jewish tradition and secular wisdom. I believed that to learn was to live. To study and study and study was to become good, and possibly great, and, in any event, to do what one (what I) was born to do. Today I can see that this deeply held faith made me what I now am: both an avid learner of Jewish texts in the style and language of the Beit Midrash, and a professor of English literature and Judaic studies. But I could not become this before I contemplated what it would be like truly to divide up Torah and *Madda,* what it would be like to live closer to total Orthodoxy, what it would be like to live closer to autonomous secularity. I had to consider these questions because there was not enough room within the Beit Midrash that I knew, the Beit Midrash that existed when I was eighteen, nineteen, twenty, or twenty-five, for a young woman who wanted to learn and some day to teach.

HOUSES OF STUDY

Binah

ותן בלבנו להבין ולהשכיל לשמוע ללמוד וללמד

לשמור ולעשות ולקים את כל דברי תלמוד

תורתך באהבה

Grant in our hearts to understand and elucidate,
    to listen, learn and teach,
To keep and to do and to fulfill
All the words of the teachings of Your Torah,
With love.

—From the morning prayer service

The path is a narrow one. Though we are free, we will travel it as if we have no choice. We will labor to become all that we have been taught to be, all that we are supposed to be. We will reach for heaven from this earth; we will be eighteen; we will be young and bright, earnest and pious, respectful of our elders, cautious in our speech, modest in our dress, restrained, thin, studious, hungry. Bending over books, imagining stars in black sky, how we will wear ourselves out in the struggle to be good. How we will spend days and nights searching for the path to forgiveness, the path to reward. . . .

. . . .

We went to Israel. We left our homes and families and traveled across the world. I thought we went looking for God. Looking for a land that had been ours before we ever knew it, had ever seen it. Looking for a people that counted us as still alive but missing in action, though we felt found, at the center of our universe. Looking for words written in black fire on top of white fire, words that would soar above us like birds pushing against the wind, and lead us to places we had never been. We tore ourselves away from everything we knew and went to a place where the streets were coarse with sand, where the sun set over the Judean desert and its mountains with the heavy, murky light of the day before creation and rose the next morning, scrubbed and smooth, like the body of a baby just born out of mess and blood, now clean and shining.

We went defenseless, not knowing we should be armed against the forces everywhere disguised as friends who were trying to persuade us that "Binah" was enough. Binah: that mysterious form of knowledge, never precisely defined, which

3

our ancient sources told us inhered in women. Binah, the ability to know one thing from out of another, *l'havin davar mitokh davar,* להבין דבר מתוך דבר. The way magicians pull endless colored scarves from one black hat, so women were supposed to know how to make little suffice, miraculously to stretch the soup, to add water yet somehow not just keep the flavor intact but enrich it. I imagine young girls and women in two long braids and pinafores, in shtetls all over Eastern Europe, being told as if it were a gift or a promise that they possessed Binah. This promise: an excuse not to teach them any more than what was absolutely necessary. We were supposed to be able to stretch our knowledge just like the soup. Binah: a war mentality. Do the best with what you have. Subsist.

But Binah was not just a myth made up by men to keep us quiet. Binah existed without them, preceded them, perplexed them, perhaps even scared them. They imagined us to be drawing ceaselessly and constantly on some well in ourselves, each woman upon her own well or upon a collective well of women's instinct. Drawing and drawing, yet never depleting it. Unlike the men, we didn't have to go anywhere to acquire our knowledge—not to yeshiva, not on a trip around the world, not even to the market. The knowledge that was destined for us, that we anticipated, was nothing outside of ourselves. It was right there beside us, the air itself seemed to whisper. In the house, in our handling of the broom, our quickness with the knife. We were to sit inside our homes, and there some angel would descend and deposit Binah inside us, perhaps without our even noticing. Unlike the men, we were never instructed to be *amelim ba'Torah,* עמלים בתורה, laboring in the study of Torah, to acquire our wisdom. We were supposed to labor bearing sons who would be *amelim ba'Torah;* we labored so that our husbands and brothers could be *amelim ba'Torah.*

However, it was our Binah and not their hard-earned wisdom that was truly necessary for survival. History had proven that it was Binah that sustained us and our families and the

Jewish people. Perhaps we acquired it mysteriously, perhaps even automatically; still we did not evade labor. The hard work came once we had acquired Binah. Binah: I heard the word and thought back to the women to whose husbands God spoke, the women with the visions, knifelike in their clarity, of what was to be done and what avoided. To Sarah, Rebecca, Esther. Women who weighed life and death in their hands as peddlers weighed fish in the market; who made fast judgments then carried out their plans; who risked their lives and their safety but never hesitated. God spoke to only one of them, spoke only once, yet to each it was as if she had heard a voice from inside and obeyed it, had seen a picture in her dreams and created it. Where Mordechai was powerless, Esther ruled a king; where Isaac was blind, Rebecca knew which son was destined to prevail; where Abraham was naive, Sarah detected real danger between his two sons. Each woman saw what had to be done; each one heard her call, unspoken though it might have been; heard it and heeded it.

I thought of those women with their visions that would not go away and imagined the heaviness of their lives. These women relied on no one, not even God Himself, to right the world, to make sure that history unfolded as planned. This responsibility for righting the world, keeping it on track: solely a woman's job. I imagined women over the centuries, down on their hands and knees in the hidden corners of the globe, on the edges of maps, scrubbing away at the world to make it the place they imagined it could be. Since they alone knew what it should look like, it became their job to change it.

I heard the echo of this word, "Binah," once more and saw myself and a circle of women standing around one well, perhaps the well at which Rebecca was found and given to Isaac, rewarded for her Binah, her knowledge of the well, with a man. I saw us standing there together, each one of us adding her own tears to the vast swell beneath us—tears of frustration, of desiring more. The mothers desiring that the reward for

Binah be something other than a blind man, that someone help them scrub the map, right the world, that the famine subside, the war end. In our own words, we were all pleading, "Not just what will suffice, but more than enough. For once, surplus." I was whispering, to God, because He was the only one I imagined would listen with sympathy, "Teach me more than I need to know. Help me find *hokhmah*, Wisdom, acquired knowledge. And let the reward for my combined Binah and *hokhmah* be something other than a good match."

....

We had arrived at the end of summer; the air was terribly hot; mosquitoes and sweat kept me from sleeping; everything I had to carry seemed too heavy. I awoke tired, dreaming of home. The summer wore on into September, and soon we knew our way to the market, to the post office, to the large American hotels where we would stop to use the phone or the pool— where we would stop to remember who we were, who our parents were, where we came from. From the boisterous streets of Jerusalem, we would hop onto these lily pads of civilization, islands of luxury, of our correctness. We yearned to be the majority once again, to dwell in a place where we spoke the language unerringly. We ordered the waiters about; we acted like our middle-aged American parents. With a wave of our hand, we refused the scarcity and the hurry of Israeli life; we sent it back to the kitchen. "Bake it some more," we ordered; "bring it back when it tastes done."

We sat in the lobbies of these hotels to be grown up, to be right, to be catered to. Because on the streets, in the eyes of the men and women passing by, in the laughs of the young soldiers on the buses, we were held as soft young Americans, spoiled, rich, selfish, immature. We served in no army; we took our time to grow up; we had a year or two years' leisure to spend in foreign countries on our parents' expense accounts, eating exotic foods, buying expensive clothes. We would go home to our America, and each Christmas we would send our small colony donations to rival the yearly incomes of the average man or woman. We were silly, naive, and careless, said the faces on the street and on the bus. We were guilty until proven innocent, kept at arm's length, suspected or ignored. My friends did not care much; I had never felt more alone.

Autumn passed without any sign from the trees. I missed the burnt orange and yellow, the flaming red leaves on the ground in front of the house, on the street, in the corners of yards. I missed the growing chill in the air, the slow, mounting excitement at winter's arrival. There were no such seasons in Israel; autumn promised nothing sweet or desirable. There was only a growing grayness, an increasing heaviness to the sky. While the rest of the country anxiously scanned the sky for signs of the first rain, I dreaded that rain and all the rains to follow. I dreaded incarceration in a place that was not home.

One day, as I was walking on the street, the rain began to fall. As it continued to fall, now faster and harder, shopkeepers came out of their stores, taxi drivers stopped their cabs, mothers ceased pushing their baby carriages. The whole city seemed to stop joyously, put out their tongues to taste this blessing, this first rain.

I watched this all and again felt invisible; over and over I was surprised that people did not attempt to walk through me as they would wade through water. That they saw me on the street and walked out of their way to avoid bumping into me. For a year, I had no body. I spoke and heard my own words, then looked for them to curl up like white smoke, rise and disappear as if they had never been spoken. Would photographs of me capture anything, I wondered. Alone, unknown, I became no one.

The land in which I was lost was a land in which people were shouting to be heard. The competition was fierce. Neither the dead nor any of the living were willing to back down, to speak softly or listen patiently for low voices obscured by dust or dark. The living were all shouting, arguing, elbowing, jostling;

I could not raise a voice, as if I knew that I had no right to speak, my bones never having been crushed against the stones that lined the paths of the city, no part of me having become stone from being in this city too long, seeing too much death inside its walls, along its outskirts. Anything I might say, a presumption, a mistake.

And the dead. In pain their throats raised the hoarsest whispers. Straining, straining, they opened their mouths, pushed their colorless lips to form words, but in vain. They could not speak; they could not save anyone from the destruction they saw as clearly as any prophet. Their words were light, too light to warn; how could I speak then and mock them like that? Caught between the living and the dead, with their sure answers and urgent messages, I was swept along the ways of Jerusalem, crowded as they must have been at times of pilgrimage, bleating sheep in the squares, men stepping heavily in the alleys.

On this path I resolved to listen. Silent, like Hannah, I prayed with no voice rising from my lips, though my lips moved faster and faster until I looked drunk. I prayed to convince myself I was living, to believe that time had not frozen to a stillness around my body. In the end, each prayer, the same prayer: a prayer for motion.

. . . .

We had school five days a week in the same building in which we lived. I lived with six other girls, the seven of us sharing a bathroom, a kitchen, three bedrooms. It was small and dirty; we decorated. We hung a red and white shower curtain and put up tinfoil in the square where there was no window, through which the workers across the way had been staring. We hung up pictures of our families and friends at home to remind us of our real lives and how we were only visiting. A resolve not to be drawn in until we would never be able to climb back out. We were here to see, to taste, to dip, tentatively, mildly, dispassionately. Not to indulge, not to love without hold, not to need the things we might find. Everything in moderation, attenuated until it cannot be seen, thinned until the flavor is too weak to be savored or even recognized.

One night early in the year, we sat in my room cutting piles of pictures from American magazines: visions of the richest, creamiest, most comforting foods. Chocolate mousse and ice cream sundaes, cups of steaming gourmet coffee, homemade apple pie, intricate berry tortes and thick layer cakes. We hung these on the peeling, scaly walls of our kitchen. Late at night, we walked to the supermarket, bought Duncan Hines cake mixes at the highest price, and came home to bake ourselves America—Teaneck, Riverdale, Skokie—our clean white kitchens sparkling with convenient appliances, our families sitting around big round tables, passing each other bowls of rice, soup, plates of chicken, fresh vegetables. To recreate for ourselves heat in the winter, air conditioning in the summer, hot water in the shower, our mothers singing us to sleep.

Our nights were long; we would pass them staring at the pictures of food or writing letters home, waiting at the end of the line for the phone, sitting on each other's beds talking. We were supposed to be studying in the Beit Midrash, the House of Study. Where was the "house of study"? One floor down from our apartment. Ten quick steps to the place that was supposed to be sacred, separate, different. An apartment just like the one in which we lived, the house of study had a bathroom, a kitchen, and three bedrooms. It seemed makeshift. Like a tent in the wilderness, our Beit Midrash seemed a substitute for the real thing, a meager offering. It was the perfect place to acquire Binah—a kitchen posing as a house of study, its disguise as convincing as an evil witch offering a rosy apple. From the Beit Midrash, we could hear the phone ringing; we would run to answer it. We would run up or down the stairs and through our unlocked doors to get another cup of coffee; distractions were welcome. We left books on our desks and disappeared for "breaks." Who could learn? With this up and down motion, this running from place to place?

Though we ran from room to room, days went by without our leaving the building. In slippers, we shuffled from our bedrooms to our kitchens to the kitchen that served as a library to the bedroom that served as a classroom. Wearing long skirts pulled over long underwear or sweatshirts pulled over pajamas, we arrived in class. We arrived to study the holiest books of our tradition. To sit before learned, esteemed teachers who had, before greeting us, awoken early, prayed, dressed children, eaten breakfast, been a part of the swift traffic on the streets. Teachers who would look at our puffy eyes and swelling faces and wonder what was wrong.

With glasses foggy from the steam of our coffee mugs, we could not see. Letters blurred; faces blurred; time washed on. The smell of indoors clung to us as I had thought it clung only to old people. The windows remained shut against the rain and the cold, and our air settled, grew weighty and thick like the gray fog outdoors, only not so fresh and not so mysterious. Shiny things were not inside; only dusty things, grimy things, slow things and heavy things. We became like those things, content among the crusty, piled-up dishes in the sink, hair in the drain, spoiled fruit on the table, ringed coffee cups wherever we looked.

The furniture seemed to hold us prisoner; our beds demanded that we sleep longer; the walls of our building became too much to resist, the stone impenetrable. What we saw out the window was only the vaguest temptation, as far away as home and comfort, certainly not calling to us, who were beyond earshot, outside of life like lepers or men about to die. Often we left the shutters closed past morning so that day was night, the first night, the longest night before promise of day, black and a sick green, like a sluggish river on the eve of storm. When would this night break, this winter, this year like a curse out of the Bible?

We should have summoned all our strength to lift ourselves up out of the mire and make our way to the Beit Midrash. Our small, gleaming library, which was a promise to me. Two narrow walls lined with shelves of books—books with brown spines, black spines, navy, maroon, gray spines with gold letters printed on them in Hebrew. The message was clear: these are words of value; if you own these books, they will make you wealthy. Heavy books, thick books, books with tiny print, spidery black letters, dense paragraphs, endless pages. Dictionaries, codes of law, the Bible, the Talmud, how-to-prepare-food-on-Shabbat books, how-to-go-to-the-mikveh books, how-to-clean-the-house-for-Passover books, histories, philosophies, fables and legends, biographies, letters, responsa, commentaries, commentaries on commentaries, prayer books. I wanted to know them all, to sweep them off the shelves, pile them into my arms until I was hugging them all to me, and run back to my room. Mine! mine! I was thinking, like a child. When can I start? Where do I start? Do I have to sleep? Who will teach me? Who wrote these books, and who has read them? What will I write, and what will I read?

I had two teachers who stretched out their hands and said, "We will take you out of here. We will take you to the place beyond walls. We will teach you what those block letters mean to us, then let you wander in the spaces between letters, in the pauses between words. We will let you write your own story, and then we will want to hear it." They were unusual women, one severe, her hair covered by a kerchief tied tightly around her head, her strong creased forehead prominent, and the other soft, a full wig of pretty brown hair on her head when she left her house, inside her house a delicate scarf sweeping back her hair.

My two teachers served God with their husbands, bowed before Him together. They taught their sons and daughters that the world is a bright, serious place; do right, keep your hand from doing any evil, serve God with your heart, your soul, your mind, of course. Live a holy life. Begin by asking every question your mind might think. Play. Talk. Study. Run in other children's neighborhoods. It was in the homes of these two women that I began to breathe again. Their lives promised me that there would be friends, that there would be a home and a mate, that there existed synagogues where women prayed instead of talked, where women would not look up from their prayer books to examine the newcomer's dress whenever the door opened, where women arrived early because they believed that was what God wanted of them, because that was what they wanted of themselves. "Don't worry," these two women said to me in their walks and their postures, "there is a place where no will tease you for trying to be good, to be better, to live as well as you can."

And when these women walked into our poor classroom, I was embarrassed. About the ways in which we lived, where we came from, what it meant to be female in this world.

. . . .

After October, I never saw the boys with whom I had gone to high school. They disappeared behind the walls of their various *yeshivot* in towns and settlements outside the city. Though we had never visited these yeshivot, my female friends and I knew what they would look like. The very sounds of their names—Har Etzion, Sha'albim, Kerem B'Yavneh—conjured images of strong, well-spoken rabbis carrying many large books at once, opening up those books with reverence and familiarity. Men reading aloud from those books in sure singsong, notes of discord in the air; great, big, light rooms with hundreds of men sitting at tables opposite each other, arguing over the interpretation of a passage, pointing to words in the books open before them, leaning back in their chairs, gesturing, waving their hands, pulling at their beards, turning red in the face in the effort to explain themselves. *Milhamta shel Torah,* מלחמתא של תורה: war for the sake of the Torah. *Kol mahloket she'hi l'shem shamayim, sofah l'hitkayem,* כל מחלוקת שהיא

לְשֵׁם שָׁמַיִם סוֹפָה לְהִתְקַיֵּים: any disagreement for the sake of heaven is destined to stand.

Learning was a war, a circumscribed war, a beautiful, passionate, and endless struggle with oneself, with others, for the purpose of getting at the truth. As if they were defending their cities, fighting dragons with swords, I imagined these boys and men studying Torah. It was the same sense of choicelessness, fervor, boyish bravery. I knew that they stayed up until late into the night arguing over words, that sleep and food were dispensable. Like Moses on Mount Sinai, they needed no food or water for sustenance; they stood and stood, opened up their mouths to drink the water that was the Torah.

That was where the boys were. Boys who had been silly in high school, who had dated casually and driven red cars, had traded in their expensive basketball shoes and their Levi's for a new look. When we would see them now, they looked thinner and older, slightly pale, as if they weren't getting enough sleep or air. They wore khaki pants and button-down shirts now, no T-shirts, and shoes instead of sneakers. They had become serious overnight. Even the ones who were not bright became absorbed by their study and left yeshiva infrequently, and then only for a few hours at a time.

I knew this because my own friends were becoming more and more distant. When we would meet, their eyes would be cloudy for the first hour until they got used to the sun and being with a girl, looking at her face, not a book. It seemed as if there was little to talk about since they were wrapped up in the web of whichever tractate they were studying. That taut, silvery web was what was most real, everything else a shadow of truth. My friend's brow is furrowed; he pretends to listen to me, though he is really thinking, "If your ox gores my ox for a second time and you still refuse to put up a fence, what is the law?" He is thinking, "Can you make a blessing over a stolen palm branch and fulfill your obligation?" I watch his face and the words rise within me: *I understand,* I want to say, *I under-*

stand what it is like to live among voices rising from yellowed pages. Trust me in that place that you have barred against me. But instead we would just see each other less and less frequently, until sitting across the table from each other was like being under water. In the space between us, words lost their beautiful fine edges, turned to long stretches of sound; soft, continuous lullabies without a meaning.

While the boys debated laws of damages, I was studying the words I had always loved—the words of the Bible. Words like land that I surveyed myself at all times, at all hours, with my own feet and hands, not trusting anyone else to do the job the way I would, to love the place like I did. The columns and columns of words, rows and rows of crops. Walking through them alone, at midnight, the moon brittle, rough and white above me.

. . . .

I met my friend Miriam on the first day of school. It was an immediate friendship. I liked the plain texture of her speech, expressions traveling slowly, bluntly across her face, her deep brown hair cut blunt. Though I had come to Israel without ever having studied Talmud, a text still closed to women in many religious institutions, including my high school, Mira had come knowing as much Talmud as any boy with whom she had studied in high school. In class, she sat at the edge of her chair, her whole body alert, toward the teacher, toward thought and speech. In her eagerness to reckon with other voices—the students, the text—she was not conscious of herself or the impressions she created. "A mind like the boys," the Talmud teacher pronounced.

While Mira studied Talmud with another girl who could read quickly and fluently, who could parse the Aramaic and see the lines of argument, Mira and I learned Bible together. Each week we prepared for class by studying the assigned passages, and each week we would offer each other half-formed guesses as to how our favorite teacher—the soft woman—might bring together all the passages into one beautiful thematic discourse. We had begun to learn her mind; we could guess which words she might find ripe with suggestion, which phrases might wind through her talk until they ended by seeming familiar as our own hands.

During lecture Mira and I sat next to each other near the front of the classroom, sharing one desk. As our teacher lifted phrases like thin threads of gold onto her fingers to make shining bridges of them, as she spoke words, now lightly, now ironically, Mira and I turned to smile slightly at each other in appreciation. We watched her transform our Beit Midrash. With her ideas and her grace, her intelligent humor and vast knowledge, she brought the *Shekhina,* the Divine Presence, into our poor room. When she bowed her head at the end of class, then thanked us, wished us a good week; when she packed her old, worn books, which she had inherited from her father, into her heavy leather carrying case, got up, and left our building, I wanted to go with her, to travel backwards in time with her, befriend her, see how she had become herself.

By December the soft woman's lecture was the only time of the week I saw Mira because she could not bear to come to any other classes. Her mind was "good as a boy's," but our classes were not. She would return from sabbaths and weekends away, having seen the boys with whom she had learned in high school, and each week, Talmud class became more of a burden to her as she marked what she was not learning, what she might have been learning. The five hours we devoted daily to Talmud could not compare with their diligent study from eight in the morning until midnight.

Our teacher chided Mira: "Think only of yourself; there is no need to compare; it isn't a race." But Mira's frustration was neither petty nor limited. It was a large, spreading thing she was battling each day. It had to do with the big, airy Beit Midrash of Har Etzion and the tiny converted kitchen where we tried to study. It had to do with what we found in those places when we arrived on our search. It had to do with that gift forced upon women, Binah, and that difficult acquisition won by men, *hokhmah*. It had to do with our hungers and our fears.

....

It had been late August when my friends and I had entered the Beit Midrash for the first time. We were greeted by silence and stagnant air; we did not tiptoe in timidly; we were not awed by the presence of long-time students too absorbed in their learning to see or hear us enter. No hands transferred the sacred books into ours. Bewildered, we picked them out of the bookshelves randomly, wondering who might have studied them before us. We looked around for clues in the ceiling, the floor, the used tables. Looked for a message, however cryptic, from the women who had preceded us, who had solved the mysteries we faced in the room wiped clean of all history. Was there any precedent for what I was about to do? Had any woman before me devoted time solely to studying Torah? Questions rose in the silent air: How do you do this? How do you spend a year, or your life, learning? When do you wake up? When do you go to sleep? How do you pray? How much time do you spend studying Talmud and how much time the Bible? What do you wear? What language do you speak? What do you discuss over meals? How do you spend your leisure time? Do you have any leisure time?

Questions and questions and few answers. These were the sorts of questions that could not be answered in speech or in writing but only in the seeing, in the sitting quietly behind someone you imagined had once been like you but was now otherwise; she had once walked into the Beit Midrash cowed and unsure, but now when she enters, all distractions fade from her sight until she sees nothing but her table and her well worn books and heads directly toward them. The knowing of a woman who lived in the thicket of voices, who had no time for food or sleep, who drank the water of Torah with great thirst and walked endless distances to sit before the wisest scholars. Where were these women? Where were they?

Once I realized that they were missing, I began to hunt for them. I found them scattered in different places: in homes with many children, each one demanding their mother; in the market, hurriedly shopping for vegetables and rugelach; at jobs, making a living; in university; in elementary schools or high schools; studying privately at their dining room tables with their own children, invited to guest lecture to women like me. Many of these women taught; many learned. But they were not in yeshiva. They laughed at the idea. Yeshiva means to sit. They had stopped sitting long ago.

....

But the fathers, the brothers, and the husbands of these women knew how to sit. These were the men who greeted my friends at Har Etzion, Sha'albim, Kerem B'Yavneh. On their first day of yeshiva, my friends were overwhelmed by the raucous argumentation over ancient laws, by the thick silence of the silent prayer, by the quick Hebrew flying in the air, by the absolute deference to the great minds of the yeshiva, rabbis and students alike. When my friends walked into the rooms I would never enter, they were young Americans with slight abilities in a place thriving and seething without them, a place that would not have minded their absence and barely noticed their presence. They saw immediately that they were guests in someone else's home. No one stroked their heads here or called them brilliant. No one asked them their opinion or their preference. They had to earn the right to ask questions of the second-year students, the fifth-year students, the tenth-year students, the rabbis, and the great rabbis.

My friends were bright; without intention, they began to observe, to eavesdrop and to spy. They learned how to dress, how to wear the same clothes over and over, unobtrusive, clean, neat, presentable, respectful. They saw that yeshiva is not a place in which to call attention to yourself intentionally. In yeshiva you wake at six, however tired you are, however cold it is in the wet, dank winter. You pray in that unmistakable early morning with the rest of the yeshiva, then you rest for half an hour or eat breakfast. Then you sit and study with your partner for a few hours, you review yesterday's class notes out loud, reread the words of the Gemara.

You cannot read slowly enough to allow your brain to travel vertically through all the information encoded in these words. Nuances of language lick like flames at your head, conflicts between two statements made by the same rabbi impress heavily upon your brain, possible resolutions tease your burdened mind, the words of a later scholar insinuate themselves into that crowded space, the context of that verse from the Bible, the reason for that commandment, a case where the punishment is not inflicted, a pun, animosity between rabbis, historical discrepancy, turn forward a page, turn back a page. . . .

All this while you are reading aloud! Sort, sort, classify, oppose, compare, contrast, infer, deduce; you are on your way. You and your partner struggle, you pull and you tug, you tease out meaning. You sit on the hard wooden chair, elbows on the table, hands at the sides of your face, fingers at temples. You work your brain trying to reconstruct. You lean back in your chair, rest for a moment, hoping that the contents of your brain will shift into a pattern you will be able to decipher.

Quick! You know you must move on, but at this moment it seems to you that no page to come will be as puzzling, as suggestive, as much your own as this one that you have just finished studying. But you discipline your sliding, yearning mind; you force yourself on into a wilderness of page, a whole new scape in which you wander gingerly, seeking to learn the terrain, the trees that grow here, the sand beneath your feet, seeking a tall gourd to shade you from the heat. This new place is hostile to you in the way that all new places are; silently they allow your entrance but offer no welcome. You have little time to learn the place; in one hour, two hours, you will be expected to appear before the monarch of this place, and he will want you to report to him on the terrain of his home, its trees, sand, shapes, and shadows; the way the sun falls at all hours of the day, the way the river feels upon your toes. All this you will have to offer him, in his language. This is what it is to prepare one page in two hours, anticipating your teacher's lesson. The fear of it, the hurry; the anxious joy of guessing at meaning; the slow, deliberate search for sense; the way you learn a new place until it seems impossible that it was ever unknown, untouchable, and mysterious as being grown up seemed when you were a child. "Welcome," you hear, "now you may stay and rest. Now you may walk as if you have a place here; you are one of us, if an enemy should come, we would defend you." Slowly you are traversing the world, stopping now in one country, now in another, hoping to see all, hoping to learn each one. This is what it is to study day after day an endless book, a book with as many pages as grains of sand, a book that great minds have finished and finished again and finished again. All you want, God, is to finish it once and begin again. Is that so much to ask? Help me finish it once, so that I may know your laws, love them, and observe them. Teach them to my children.

There is so much you want, and how will you achieve it? You think of the story you learned in high school, of the rabbi who has become familiar in your dreams, whom you see when you close your eyes in prayer on the Day of Atonement, the rabbi who ate solely to say the blessings praising God, acknowledging whose world it is. You think of the great scholar who came to the end of his life and could account for every moment of his life but ten; you think of the martyrs, skin flayed, thirsty, speaking faith forever. You think of the boys who died for the land on which you walk daily and their mothers ripping their hair over their sons' graves; you think of the six million dead without names. Without graves. Without places to haunt seeking comfort. You think of the chill silence in which you left your mother yesterday; you think of the cruel words you said to your brother; you think of how you laughed at the poor teacher and how he blushed and fled the room; you remember the grandmother to whom you don't write often enough. You are drowning in acts of commission and omission; the sky weighs down upon you.

Back to the page. Because if you think like this too long, you will lose the page forever; you will try to climb straight walls, break iron bars before windows.

....

So the days go in yeshiva? You dedicate your will; you forget there is a world; you don't leave; you get up seldom; you question and you wonder; you desire. You watch your teachers silently and you despair. Untouchable. You can't talk to them; you can't confess to them; you can't aspire to be like them. They take up your whole world—width, breadth, height. Giant men wearing the sun like a necklace. You look at them now and they are men; again, and they are prophets; again, and their heads turn to silver crowns and their legs to the wooden handles of the Torah scroll. Dense bodies, rounded with the layers they wear: shirts, vests, jackets; underneath all these, *tallit katan* (fringes). As protected as a Torah scroll in all its velvet coverings. You treat them with the same deference, the same humility you grant that scroll, because it seems they are its living form. It seems that scroll belongs to them.

And now you must study so that you will not be caught unprepared in class, so that you will not disappoint your teacher, embarrass yourself, cheat yourself of the insights he will share, whose value you will know only if you have labored first. You close your mind to everything but the page; there is no other way. Inside words and phrases spin in your mind, their shards landing in your speech, your notes. For a second, you sense meaning, elusive as a shot of light in an oil puddle; perhaps it is not even the meaning itself you sense, but its presence, the way you might know there is a secret without knowing what it is. Instantly you go after this hint, try to enlarge it, make it real. You toss it into your partner's hands like a slippery fish; he tries vainly to catch. Begin again. And again. Until the ideas are there; until they are pared down; until words are sharp and precise; until you have charts, columns, order.

Then it is time for lunch. After lunch, you sleep. When you wake up, you pray. After you pray, you return to the Beit Midrash, this time for class. You try to keep up; as if you are a child holding his mother's hand at a great outdoor fair, you chase after her, threading through crowds. But somehow you have wandered from your dream into a terrifying nightmare; your mother is no longer who you thought she was; she doesn't care if you stay by her side; if you get lost, she won't stop, won't slow down, won't search for you when dusk descends. Your teacher is this unnatural mother. Don't expect him to hold your hand; don't expect him to look down at his side and see your short legs straining to keep up with his long strides.

Still in class. You follow the teacher's known voice, its ups and downs. Questions, answers, propositions, refutations, conclusions. You flip back and forth in the book before you as he flips back and forth in his mind. If you stop to marvel, you are lost. After some months, you may learn his voice well. You may know when to concentrate and when you may let your straining mind rest. Sometimes you will persevere; you will come to the end with your teacher, look around you astonished, wondering how you came to the place in which you find yourself. Then you and your partner will run off to your desk without speaking; you will try to make a fire from the slightest twigs; you will cup your hand around this weak flame to shield it from the wind, blow on it yourself with tenderness and care; you will guard it and contribute to it, sit by it beside the night, vigilant.

There will be times of triumph and times of failure, times when you will lose your patience, and, helpless, become frustrated beyond reason. Sometimes you are content to sit and watch the seconds, minutes, quarter hours, tick by on your wristwatch. Sometimes you can only sleep.

In late afternoon, you put away your Talmud. You take out the codes of law or a book from the Prophets or a book of medieval philosophy, and you study that with a different partner. If you are among the younger students, maybe with someone older; if you are among the older students, maybe with someone younger. You study, you slow down, your mind begins to wander; it is time for dinner. You eat the same food you ate last week and will eat next week; you talk, you pretend to talk. Then you have some time to yourself in the room you share with two others.

. . . .

And then the last round of the day: night study. You stay in one place, your place; you stay and you stay, as if you were guarding something. In the beginning the Beit Midrash is full, crowded even. Men sit in pairs; they lean back in their chairs as they have not done all day. The study is less rigorous, the air less electric. After a full day, minds are just now fully open, susceptible to impression. The feeling is of good fellowship. The hours pass this way, sweet and round.

As the night gets later, the Beit Midrash empties. Outside it is night, black, silent. Outside it is still; the wind weaves between the trees; you might hear a baby's cry, distant and diffuse, or a lone truck on the gravel road. Everything is quiet, slow. And still you are studying. And by now even your study partner has gone to sleep, and men are sitting singly around the room, which has become much larger and emptier. And you continue to sit because you know—you have heard and you can tell it is true—that the later you study, the more yeshiva is your home, the place that claims you. When you come back in the morning to your seat and you have been gone only a few hours, the walls, your chair, the table, and the books seem to whisper a welcome, honor you, and entreat you. In the day, you see the other few men who wait up as you do; you nod your heads to each other slightly because you are linked now; you all know the joy and the dizziness of that holy study—as if you have been fasting for days on end and have passed through the fierce hunger and pain into brilliant, blinding light. You come to the end of night weightless and buoyant. What does your haggard body matter, the dark gray rings under red eyes? You have passed beyond tiredness; you have raced with exhaustion and won.

There are nights when you leave the Beit Midrash, that too large, unpeopled haven, for a smaller place. In night, you begin to feel small. Sitting by the great glass windows that look out onto nothing but blackest night, you open your book. And you have left the argumentation of day and the straining to impress human beings, and you are in the time that matters now. You are alone and you might speak to God. You turn to books written by great men who doubted and questioned and struggled as you struggle too; you read and then you put your head down. You are still. For a moment you sleep, then you wake; you read three lines; you are thinking and praying and breathing softly all at once. You believe at these times. All the things that you can never believe by the glare of day, you can accept now, this soothing, soothing time. This time when God is watching over you, covering you as you sleep, guarding you as you drift between sleep and wakefulness, dream and prayer, as you descend to meet the truth of yourself, your goodness, the place from which you pray. The night is your home, as is the darkness; all space is God's, and there is not enough room for Him in this world.

And now after nights like these, many nights like these, now yeshiva is your home, as much as it is anyone's. Your home—the place you run to, that you return to, that protects you; where your mind lives and your body longs to be.
. . . .
You have a mind and you have a heart and you have a soul. Your mind is busy with the study, dissection, understanding.

Your heart is weeping for your sins, the rewards and gifts you receive undeserving. And you wonder why this good is yours, and you feel your life a blessing of the thinnest gold. And always you are wondering: Where have these angels come from who deliver me in safety, who pluck me from grave danger? Where have they come from, and why have they come to me? Why do I have everything when most of the world hungers and dies, languishes from loneliness, shrivels in desolation? My heart is weeping for the ones who have nothing. In vain I scan the street, looking for the poor beggar, the prophet in disguise, with rags on his back and bundles in his torn hands and a dirty cap on his head. I wait for him to appear, to make the miracles we don't believe in anymore and hand the hungry people two loaves of thick, warm bread for the Sabbath and shiny fish just caught from the sea and three heavy gold coins to warm in their palms, to wrap in soft cloth. My soul is begging like the people on the street; my soul is poor, cold, huddled against the wind. My soul is caught in this world, where you have to give up hopes and plans and live normally, where you have to eat and sleep and remain silent when you have too much to contain. My soul is longing to escape; it knows of another place, of ecstasy and flight; it pushes inside me; it pushes with a force that I cannot ignore, that I ward away; then I cry when it is gone. My soul is forever being born, always dying.

. . . .

And so I imagined a world for my friends inside the small sturdy settlements that held their yeshivot. Temptation, desire to be there too. To be neat and tall and perfect, not to need food, drink, or sleep. To grow thin, even gaunt. To yield body to soul, soul to God; to be conscious of nothing except the words, the teacher, your God. Forget your body, forget your face, live like an unnamed creature.

Nourished by a place that is looking to glorify you, that is looking to make you, how easily you could lose your imperfections, your irregularities and aberrations; how easily you could give yourself like the choicest sacrifice to some weak vision because prophecy is not to be questioned. Abraham heard a voice tell him to slaughter the son he loved: child of laughter. He obeyed; in that moment Isaac died, his soul flew away and hid among the bushes; the world tottered. As it was righting itself, Sarah died. She heard the story in its barest bones; she heard a voice telling her that the son she had borne of her old age, protected from rivals, raised to be strong and brave and to persevere, that son had been strapped motionless to an altar by her husband, the man who had known her body all these years, known it the night Isaac was first thought of. Sharp knives, thick ropes, hidden spots. The voice whispering this awful story to Sarah continues. Though she is clasping her hands over her ears; it tells her that in the last second, an angel seized Abraham's hand. An angel, Sarah is thinking, of all things, an angel!

She is reeling, nauseous, dizzy. Her son almost dead, almost cut to pieces, almost, almost. Echo, echo, echo, echo. Among the mountains and the stones, in the wind, the trees. She cannot run far enough from this terror, the terror of almost. The tightrope terror, the panic of closeness, of small differences, of what could so easily have been if not for an angel, if not for the least likely interference, the chancest encounter. So she dies, Sarah. Dies of this fear, of what her own hands could do and she unable to stop them. Of what might happen, at all times, at any time. She dies of the thinness of the thread.

The world was spattered with blood on that day. And no one to clean it up. It was death—death of a ram, death of a father, of a mother, of laughter, of a child—all upon the altar.

What we sacrifice to callings we are not even sure we have heard. What we give up for the faintest possibilities.
. . . .
We went to Israel. We left our homes and traveled across the world. I thought we went looking for God. Looking for a land

that had been ours before we had ever seen it. Looking for a people; looking for the words written in black fire upon white fire. Our passion went unnoticed.

This gift of feeling that cannot be bought nor induced, heeds no beckoning and accepts no bribe—gone like a thing of no value.

Prophet in beggar's clothes; once he has left the town unsung, how we go rushing after him to bring him back in glory. Everyone knows he can never be found again.

············

The desire with which we had come looking for God, a land, a people, our words—this rich and many-colored flame singled itself into a strong but ordinary passion for becoming grown up, a fire to be women. The time for loving God had passed us by. We were restless and discomfited, no longer able to pray giving away our souls, losing our bodies in the sway. We did not have the peace of mind you need in order to believe with all the strength that is yours, trusting in the darkness and the silence. We could not find the times in which letters float together mystically to form words. We missed the ecstasy, the out-of-body; we could not put our hands on the hard skeletons of thought, belief, and passion. We were not solitary enough, not silent or disciplined enough, to receive the blessing of the blue-black hours that are meant to be spent alone, on the edge of sleep, hovering over the void, waiting for creation.

And more than that. How conscious we were of eyes always upon us, of judgments that might be inscribed as we moved. So we walked with straight backs, as if our mothers had set heavy books on our heads and told us to cross the room, eyes fastened on some invisible point ahead of us. If it had been God's burning, focused gaze that awed and silenced us, I would have understood. I would have rejoiced that God was real and that His gaze was powerful. But it was not God's eyes that we feared, and it was not from Him that we hid the secrets of our hearts out of fear or shame. How far we were from that privileged, hard-earned step where God is real, present in a different way than anything we had ever known.

We were caught below in the world of the body, parading before a line of boys and men, only one of whom had to want us. If only we were thin and beautiful and pious enough to win this Jacob to our tents. This was as far as our thought went: if only. But what would happen if only? Then would we be peaceful enough to pray again as we had when we were fourteen? Or might we have forgotten by then how to pray and why we ever prayed to begin with? Was there a chance that by then we might be settled and matronly, relying on the piety of our husbands to fill our tents with light? Wordlessly, we claimed weakness. Our frames could not stand the intensity of a rising spirit, so we renounced our souls and gave ourselves over to bodies.

Even as our passion breathed and died, the boys' was being born. The boys were in yeshiva. The boys were growing strong. The boys were pushing their minds, straining their bodies, until they dropped in exhaustion. The girls, though, were in their rooms. The girls were weak with imagination, weak with worry, haunted by nightmares. The girls are young, playing with dolls, dressing them up, making false gods, hiding them among their belongings. With the cruelty of children, the girls are stuffing these dolls, dressing them, throwing them callously into a bag and taking them to the streets to peddle. Looking for someone who will buy. The girls are playing dress-up; they walk leisurely into town, try on hats on the street, play with colored scarves, wrap them around their heads. They set up tiny kitchens, set up house, play house, imagine what it is to have a house of their own, imagine what it is to be married, what it is to be a grown-up. The girls begin to be afraid that no one will have them. In their minds, they begin to grow old, to wither. They put on consciousness and determination; they put on purpose; they stride out the doors of their own yeshiva into the center of town. They will find someone for the doll they have crafted, the doll that they will peddle, the doll that is themselves.

....

Leah was our nightmare, haunting our dreams, appearing as we turned winding corners in Jerusalem; as dusk descended, she was there, obstructing our path always. Unwanted woman, dowdy sister, soft-eyed burden. Left holding the flowering roots, left with enough sons to have made any woman happy. How she would have laughed at Hannah's sorrow—Hannah, the woman with the man, but childless. Hannah—the gracious womanly woman whose husband pleads with her, "Is my love not greater than the worth of ten sons?" Hannah—beloved wife, fitted to her husband's body, finally triumphant, bearing him his son, the prophet. Luckless Leah—unimportant mother of the unimportant sons.

The story continues to tell itself to us. In a whisper, a hush, the Torah of seventy faces, infinite faces, offers up this face to us again and again until it becomes written on our own faces, until others can see it written there. The story of Leah and Rachel. It inscribes itself, a needle pulling a tough thin thread in its wake. A glinting silver needle, matching the knife of the Sacrifice. This needle sews the story into our skin so that we cannot lose it, so that when we give birth, the stitches will groan and stretch, then settle back into place, taut, invisible. And the warning is: *Look sharp, be on your guard, don't turn into Leah.* Leah, the terror of our dreams; we fear her the way we feared as children, tasting fear on our tongues, unable to wash the taste from our mouths. At night she possesses the dark caves of our minds, blocking the light so that when it does come, it comes fitted to her shape, lighting her from the sides, from behind, so that she is like a dreadful candle, sputtering and ghoulish, flaring without warning.

From out of these dark dreams, we call to Rachel, who seems to each one of us to belong to us before anyone else, who seems to each one of us to be our real mother, our true mother. Of the Four, the one who is most mother. Young and pretty, the one who listens and understands, is desired by men not her husband, envied by the wives of those men, coveted by their daughters. We ask her to adopt us, to bequeath to us her fate, blot out the fate of her sister.

But we are still young, still daughters, not yet mothers, not yet friends of mothers. The rest of Rachel's story remains mysterious and hidden. We don't know and we can't guess what lies on the other side of desire, envy, and coveting; we can't begin to imagine the steadfast well of loneliness from which a married woman draws, to which she adds. We cannot imagine who Rachel is when she is not being our mother, we who do not know yet what it is to be a woman.

. . . .

This year: a time in which we were girls one minute and young women the next, and then girls again, and then young women. A time in which we missed our mothers with an ache that kept us awake in our beds, yet by morning we imagined ourselves laughing behind carriages, exchanging stories among mothers. We were dressing ourselves as women; we were noticing our bodies; we were thinking we knew desire. We wanted to be held, consoled, loved passionately, warmly, tenderly, the way our mothers had loved us, the way we imagined men loved women. We set about to become women for whom some Jacob would work for fourteen years, years that in his eyes, in his love, would seem like days.

Like Rebecca before us, we rode out into scorched desert on camels, our hands shielding our eyes from the sun, looking out into the distance for this man, the intended one, looking for the man who was looking for a mother and a lover. We too were looking for a mother and a lover and children. We wanted echoes absorbed by the heat of arid lands, by the cloth of our tents.

We ride on, pay no attention to the sun. We are willing, we are more than willing to leave our past behind, to abandon our former homes to be plundered. We are willing to be plundered ourselves, to be seized. We want that even.

Now as if we have arrived at some magical point that we recognize as if we have arrived here before, we stop moving and sit alert and silent on our camels, watching the landscape. Waiting for him to appear against it as if he comes from nowhere, as if he were conceived by us, born and nourished within our minds alone, so that now when he comes to meet us, it is as if he comes toward us from some place within ourselves, a place we know intimately, the back of our vision, the birthplace of our dreams. Ahead we see the vast stretches that we have never traveled before; they look smooth as sky, as sand, as the sea from a distance.

When he comes near, we will be ready to fall from our placid obedient animals. We will be ready to rise up from the ground gracefully, lift our scarves on our fingertips and cover our warm faces modestly to keep them covered. We will be ready to follow him to the place we cannot see from where we are, the place that he will show us.

....

By the end of the year I was no longer scared of becoming Leah. I had been chosen by my own Jacob. As I remember him now, it seems that we were always in the synagogue or on the way to the synagogue. It was always the Sabbath or close to the Sabbath or a fast day or a holy day. We spoke in a language that was rich enough to give us all the words we needed and did not know how to say. One night as we did not touch each other, according to the law, he said to me in the dark that he believed he was beginning to understand what our Sages meant when they said that God loved Israel with a "greater affection." Silently, we agreed,

We will walk to the synagogue together, in the morning when it is still cold and our feet in sandals feel the chill, and in the evening too. When we get there, we will go our separate ways— you to the side of the women and I to the side of the men; then I will shut my eyes and pray to God, and you will shut your eyes and pray to God. We will sit miles from each other at these times, and it will be as if we are in different worlds, and in some way that I cannot explain to you now, we will meet there, in the place where God accepts the song of our prayers, and He will listen to our voices at the same time as they wrap and twist around each other, braiding one thought, one strong wish, one need.

Then he would be gone, having left me to enter on his side, close his eyes, and search for his God as he had said he would. And I was meant to be searching for my God at that time. But somehow I never was. Always I was watching him, hurrying to my seat so that I might see him enter in his quiet, modest, beautiful way and find his row, the row where he sat each week with his brothers and father; watching him slide in quietly, sit down in his place, the way I imagined he entered the Beit Midrash in his yeshiva, with dignity, unaware of eyes upon him, unaware of how much his seat was his, how he approached it singlemindedly, as if it drew him near, never guessing how much each place he chose seemed to belong to him.

Then, as always, he would open his prayer book and begin to move his lips, close his eyes and draw into himself until the world around him was gone. I would watch the fathers point him out to their young sons, and I would notice the girls huddle together and look at him admiringly and look at me then too, wondering at our having found each other, chosen each other.

As the evening prayers go on, I try to look away from him, try to find myself. I turn my face, shut my eyes; still I continue to see him, see his profile, see the shape of his thin fingers holding the closed book, notice the light as it falls on his hair and arms each week at this hour. The rhythm of my body's rock becomes the rhythm of his body's, the speed of my prayer, the speed of his. I cannot imagine being in this room without him.

I am confident all this time that he is not thinking of me. Confident that he is thinking of his sins, his strivings, his promises and betrayals. Why is it, I am wondering, that he can leave me for a time, speak to his God, and then return to me, meet me by the flowers, cleansed and pure, ready for the next day, the next week, when I have not found time for God since I met him? In all the hours we have spent at the synagogue, in all the time poring over holy books together, never have I been nearing my God. All I have been conscious of is the shape of his hands and the smell of his body and the imagined texture of his hair. How shocked he would be to know how I have abandoned God for him. He would send me away; he would not understand.

One Sabbath, he had led the congregation in prayer. On that day, he had stood before the Ark and held the Torah in its velvet covering pressed close to his body, the way he could not press me to his body. He had held the Torah and so quietly that I wondered if I had actually heard his voice or only imagined it, whispered the words *Shema Yisrael, Adonai Eloheinu, Adonai Ehad:* "Hear, O Israel, the Lord is our God, the Lord is One." Though I had said these words and heard them all my life, they seemed in that instant to become lost to me. I had found a man who spoke to me, who was there beside me, undeniable in his body; bones and muscles and sinews and skin and eyes that did not compromise, did not yield; and what is a soul without a body?

Little by little, I lost more things, lost faster. The words I have loved as my own had stopped being beautiful because I found them beautiful; instead I loved them because he spoke them. The joy of the holidays was seeing him. The heavy, thick-spined books were cherished not because of the secrets and promises they held but because he gave them to me as gifts, inscribed in his thin, meticulous handwriting, which I recognized as if it were my own.

....

Shavuot came, the holiday for celebrating the gift of the Torah. In the darkness between night and morning, he and I walked to the Western Wall. We walked the old, old Jerusalem streets in near silence. The gift of the Torah, God's gift, hovering above us: a mountain, a cloud, a wellspring, a rock.

We walked silent and hopeful, my hands at my sides, his at his own. Nothing was braided; everything was ready for the braiding. When the Torah was given, fire and billows of smoke came with it. The shaking of the earth, the shaking of the people of Israel. Tablets, a scroll, knowledge, and a tradition to hand down: hands to hands to hands to hands.

My hands were empty as we walked, and they were still empty when I returned to America. Perhaps I had found my Jacob, but I had not neared finding my God, and I had almost given away the words of black fire written upon white. A year that might have been the gain of those words, our God, a land: gone, not to be recovered. The gleaming books in the library, unlearned, unpossessed.

Looking for Jacob, we had hidden from God, then God had hidden too, gone like the prophet in beggar's clothes. We had hidden and found solace and ease in what already belonged to us, what we would not have to work for, or search for or fight for: Binah, that old gift, bequeathed to us from the air, the sea, the sky, the teachers who invoked it, the Beit Midrash that housed it. *Hokhmah*—the chance to range freely in our minds, hearts, and souls—flew away like the soul of Isaac as he lay upon the altar.

....

Houses of Study

Love comes in at the eye.—w. b. yeats, *"A Drinking Song"* (1916)

Ann Arbor, 1978

I t was my paternal grandfather who wore glasses. In 1933 in the European libraries that had allowed her in, Grandma Ann held a ruler for him beneath one faint line of manuscript, then another, and painstakingly he copied what he saw. Sometimes she held one manuscript and he another, and he discovered and deciphered the differences. My father told me that at the time of Grandpa Harry's death in 1981, he was legally blind.

Legally blind: what did this mean? I wondered. He was able to see, but only when he wore his glasses. His prescription was dramatic, extreme. As radical as he was quiet. I always imagined that I had eyes like his because I got glasses at such a young age, in second grade. They were brown and ordinary, and with them my mother bought me a book called *Katie's Magic Glasses*. On the pages before the glasses all the illustrations were fuzzy; you had to squint to imagine what they were supposed to be representing. On the pages after the glasses, the images were clear.

The world wasn't magic; it hadn't changed a bit. The magic belonged to the round lenses in frames twisting around Katie's ears and resting on her nose. But if I put on my own glasses, the fuzzy images in the book got no clearer. So there did exist a fuzziness that would not go away, that no magic could resolve.

Perhaps that was blindness—the refusal of the world to come into focus, no matter what you did. From fuzziness, it simply disappeared. Those were the pages before Katie's book began. Nothingness, blackness, *tohu va'vohu*, תהו ובהו, wild and waste—words whose only sense was rhyme, not representation. Churning water overflowing the no-boundaries of the no-world. It was only what other words could describe, and it was not that either.

The pages before the fuzziness were my grandfather's eyes, or the eyes of a child not yet born, not yet thought of.

Knowing about my grandfather, I felt my sight a privilege that might at any moment be rescinded. And with it, all the books. When our mother was busy, my younger brother and sister, Jonathan and Naomi, would come to me, books in hand. I had once been dependent on others to read to me too. Returning would be a curse. I understood that it would be slower than any slowness I had ever suffered, that it would be as if I had asked someone else to eat for me or sweat for me.

I would never be able to read Braille with my fingers. Reading *meant* seeing: the image of the word, the extraordinary quickness with which the word slid into the next word, having already imprinted itself on the screen of the brain. How the words translated into knowledge was a mystery. Each girl about whom I read was a black and white typesetter, smeared with ink. The dress and smock of each girl in each book were forever soiled; their boot soles swam in smarmy black rivers. They had to do with blackness and print, with a grainy whiteness and paper. Emily, Anne, Laura, Mary, Jo, Beth, Marmie: words swept into shape, miracle beings every one.

Negligible in terms of size, each character was a conception, a pile of words turning from dust into gold, back to dust. The gold—the *sense,* the impression of a character as a full being, an entity—was the result of reading to yourself, a process so private even you could not understand it. The flight of the word to the eye to the brain. The translation of what was outside yourself into your deepest parts, the seat of knowledge, of certainty that one knew what one was talking about.

My grandfather had died from heart failure, but never could I separate his death from his blindness. It seemed to me he had died of the death of his eyes. He had died of not being able to see, and so, not being able to read.

....

Grandpa Harry was an author. Though he worked all his life as a teacher and his books were textbooks and scholarly monographs, he was the closest I had come to meeting a writer. His books were published, sold, and bought; he fought with the publishers over what were called "royalties." Though when I heard the word "writer," I thought of Judy Blume and Beverly Cleary, somehow I imagined my grandfather sitting with them, in a circle, small and tight.

His famous book was *Ivrit Hayah, Modern Hebrew: A First-Year Course in Conversation, Reading and Grammar.* People would come up to my father in synagogue and say, "I learned to read Hebrew from your father's book." Every synagogue library and every afternoon school seemed to have copies. My friends' parents would often have a dusty one with a dull red or blue spine; it was the precise blue of the Birnbaum *siddur,* the standard American prayer book. You could mistake one for the other. Though "font" was not a word we knew then, the font was the same, and the books weighed alike. Their covers, a cotton weave become quickly shaggy, felt the same.

My grandfather's book was published in New York in 1946, two years before Israel became a state. Part Two followed in 1952, and in 1963, seven years before I was born, the revised edition came out.

Hebrew is both a modern and an ancient language. Some day if you have the good fortune to visit Israel, you will observe how the tongue of the prophets has been reborn on the lips of young and old. Hebrew, now a living language, is spoken in the homes and in the schools, in the factories and on the farms, in the cities and settlements of Israel. As one author picturesquely described it, "Airplanes as well as angels now fly through Hebrew literature."

VI

אֱלִיעֶזֶר בֶּן יְהוּדָה

מִלּוֹן

will build	יִבְנֶה (ע׳ בָּנָה)	Eliezer ben Yehudah	אֱלִיעֶזֶר בֶּן יְהוּדָה
will understand	יָבִינוּ (ע׳ הֵבִין)	Paris	פָּרִיז נ׳
that unites	הַמְאַחֶדֶת	medicine	תּוֹרַת הָרְפוּאָה נ׳
to change	לַהֲפֹךְ	stopped	חָדַל
in the beginning	בַּתְּחִלָּה	pogroms	פְּרָעוֹת נ.ר.
was born (m.)	נוֹלַד	were slain	נֶהֶרְגוּ
spread	הִתְפַּשֵּׁט	felt (v.)	הִרְגִּישׁ
speech	דִּבּוּר ז׳	thought of	עָלָה בְלִבּוֹ
		Europe	אֵירוֹפָּה נ׳

The story of the man who revived Hebrew as a spoken language.

לִפְנֵי שִׁשִּׁים שָׁנָה הָיְתָה הַלָּשׁוֹן הָעִבְרִית כְּלָשׁוֹן מֵתָה. רַק אֲנָשִׁים מְעַטִּים דִּבְּרוּ עִבְרִית.

וּבַיָּמִים הָהֵם הָיָה נַעַר צָעִיר בְּשֵׁם אֱלִיעֶזֶר. תַּלְמִיד הָיָה בְּאוּנִיבֶרְסִיטָה בְּפָרִיז וְלָמַד רְפוּאָה, כִּי רָצָה לִהְיוֹת לְרוֹפֵא. וְהַנַּעַר הַזֶּה אָהַב אֶת הַלָּשׁוֹן הָעִבְרִית מְאֹד וְלֹא חָדַל לִקְרֹא בִּסְפָרִים עִבְרִיִּים יוֹם וָלַיְלָה.

וּפִתְאֹם פָּרְצוּ הַפְּרָעוֹת הַנּוֹרָאוֹת בְּרוּסְיָה. הַרְבֵּה יְהוּדִים נִפְצְעוּ וְנֶהֶרְגוּ. צַר הָיָה לַתַּלְמִיד אֱלִיעֶזֶר. הוּא הִרְגִּישׁ בְּצַעַר עַמּוֹ וְרָצָה לַעֲזֹר לָהֶם, אֲבָל מַה יָּכֹל לַעֲשׂוֹת?

[293]

From *Modern Hebrew*, by Harry Blumberg and Mordecai H. Lewittes. Story VI: Eliezer Ben-Yehudah Revives the Jewish Language.

וְהִנֵּה עָלָה בְּלִבּוֹ רַעְיוֹן גָּדוֹל: יָשׁוּב הָעָם הָעִבְרִי לְאַרְצוֹ,
אֶרֶץ יִשְׂרָאֵל. שָׁם יִחְיֶה בְּכָבוֹד וּבְלִי פַּחַד, יַעֲבֹד וְיִבְנֶה.
אֲבָל אִם יָשׁוּבוּ הָעִבְרִים לְאַרְצָם, אֵיךְ יָבִינוּ זֶה אֶת זֶה? הֵם
צְרִיכִים בְּלָשׁוֹן אַחַת שֶׁכֻּלָּם יוֹדְעִים. וּמַה הִיא הַלָּשׁוֹן הָאַחַת
הַמְאַחֶדֶת אֶת כָּל הָעִבְרִים? הֲלֹא הִיא הַלָּשׁוֹן הַהִיסְטוֹרִית
שֶׁלָּהֶם–עִבְרִית! וְעִבְרִית הָיְתָה כְּלָשׁוֹן מֵתָה. (historic)
וֶאֱלִיעֶזֶר נִשְׁבַּע לַהֲפֹךְ אֶת הַלָּשׁוֹן הַמֵּתָה לְלָשׁוֹן חַיָּה.
הוּא לֹא רַק אָמַר כִּי אִם גַּם עָשָׂה.

הוּא נָסַע לְאֶרֶץ יִשְׂרָאֵל וְהִתְחִיל לְדַבֵּר רַק עִבְרִית
לְאִשְׁתּוֹ, אֲשֶׁר בַּתְּחִלָּה לֹא הֵבִינָה אֲפִילוּ מִלָּה אַחַת.

נוֹלַד לָהֶם בֵּן וְהֵם דִּבְּרוּ אֵלָיו רַק עִבְרִית. הַמִּשְׁפָּחָה שֶׁל
בֶּן יְהוּדָה הָיְתָה הַמִּשְׁפָּחָה הָעִבְרִית הָרִאשׁוֹנָה בְּאֶרֶץ יִשְׂרָאֵל.
וְגַם לְכָל הַחֲבֵרִים שֶׁלָּהֶם דִּבְּרוּ רַק עִבְרִית.

אָמְרוּ לָהֶם הַחֲבֵרִים: "מְשֻׁגָּעִים אַתֶּם! לֹא תוּכְלוּ לַהֲפֹךְ
לָשׁוֹן מֵתָה לְלָשׁוֹן חַיָּה!" אֲבָל אֱלִיעֶזֶר וְאִשְׁתּוֹ לֹא שָׂמוּ לֵב
אֲלֵיהֶם.

עָבְרוּ שָׁנִים וְעוֹד מִשְׁפָּחוֹת בִּירוּשָׁלַיִם הִתְחִילוּ לְדַבֵּר
עִבְרִית. וּמִירוּשָׁלַיִם הִתְפַּשֵּׁט הַדִּבּוּר הָעִבְרִי בְּכָל אֶרֶץ
יִשְׂרָאֵל, וּמִשָּׁם עָבַר לְאֵירוֹפָּה וְלַאֲמֵרִיקָה.

סוֹף סוֹף בָּא הַחֲלוֹם הַגָּדוֹל שֶׁל אֱלִיעֶזֶר בֶּן יְהוּדָה.
הַלָּשׁוֹן הַהִיסְטוֹרִית שֶׁל הָעָם הָעִבְרִי הָיְתָה עוֹד פַּעַם לְלָשׁוֹן
חַיָּה בְּפִי הָעָם.

[294]

My father had grown up in Brooklyn with a father whom he believed to be a master of one language and one language only: Hebrew. When children came to play, my father volunteered to translate between them and his father, taking ideology for reality. At the few baseball games my grandfather attended with his son, he sat with a copy of *Davar*, the Israeli newspaper that he could buy in "the States." By 1968, when my grandparents left America for Israel, he had succeeded in establishing Modern Hebrew as an academic discipline at Hunter College, where he taught.

Israel for me was the land where they lived; I knew the blue and white flag with its star in the center, and I knew their address: Rehov Beit HaKerem 28. In my room at home I had a box where I kept letters. My grandfather's letters were written in Hebrew, penned by a shaky hand, addressed from Jerusalem to Ann Arbor, where we lived. The address of both destination and origin were in English; this puzzled me since the mailmen on Rehov Beit HaKerem could read only Hebrew. How could such a letter find its way out of Israel? The stamps were Israeli; this puzzled me too since such a letter had to travel *within* America as well as to America.

My grandfather's letters were rare, and they took fourteen days to arrive, but they rarely dealt in passing time, so the delay was unimportant. In Hebrew, he wanted to know what I was studying; he wanted to correct a sentence I had miswritten or a verb I had conjugated almost correctly but not quite. While I was living in the three-tense world of story and action, he was living in the time-stopped drama of my linguistic education, where events were not so vital as the capability of describing them aptly and specific detail could yield to a motto or phrase that might come in handy later for reuse.

I wrote my letters; he corrected them and sent them back. From the hand of his postman in the shady, still cobblestoned roads of Jerusalem to the hand of our postman in Ann Arbor, a town still surrounded by corn fields, the lessons were transmitted. The envelope and its stamp were the miraculous holders of the time that had elapsed and the space traversed.

It was a flowery Hebrew Grandpa Harry wrote, a Hebrew still in disbelief that airplanes flew through Hebraic skies, that washers and driers, parking lots and sports teams, telephones and radios, theaters and restaurants, post offices and department stores, now possessed full vocabularies. His letters betrayed few of those modernities. When he sent greetings on a birthday or end-of-year celebration, he wrote the antique formula *mi yiten,* מי יתן, if only good things might come to pass. When he wanted to express consternation or sorrow, he wrote *tzar li,* צר לי, how sorrowful it is to me, the words of King Saul upon the death of Jonathan. Tense and person seemed the subject matter of the letters; vowels and prepositions conveyed love.

In my school in Ann Arbor in the 1970s the love of language looked different. In Hebrew, as in English, we had no grammar books. Unlike our workbooks, which we got to keep at the end of the year, that we could write our names in, that were *ours,* my grandfather's hard-cover book left no room for a student to pencil in answers. It did not seem to anticipate a student in the same way; we were interchangeable with all the other students who would inherit the old, used book. In this way, the book, like my grandfather, came from a past era, in which books were a sign of wealth, ownership was rare, and pens remained aloof from sacred page.

Unlike the vivid materials that comprised my education, my grandfather's textbook offered no color pictures. The children in the black and white snapshots were all dressed neatly in white shirts and matching pants and skirts; they held flags. Pioneers danced the hora against vast expanses of mountain and valley; a woman in shorts plowed a field with a metal implement; old Jews leaned against the Wailing Wall; the Hebrew University sat atop Mount Scopus, a barren sepia vista in the distance; an El-Al plane stood waiting on a runway; Jews and Arabs labored together.

When it came to the stories, they were short. There were no characters you could get to know. A mixture of folk tales, historical anecdotes, Talmudic and Biblical personages, contemporary situations, moral lessons, the mishaps of the wise men of Chelm mixed with the advice of King Solomon, and the story of the building of a Jewish port in Tel Aviv introduced the journeys of the medieval poet Yehudah Ha-Levi. You could read of students in a Hebrew class who founded a Hebrew club and convinced everyone to talk only Hebrew, even though they lived in America, while on the next page, you could follow a short legend written by Benjamin Franklin translated into biblical Hebrew. This extra-Midrashic legend imagined Abraham hosting a nonbeliever, learning tolerance for all peoples. In later chapters, you might read about Jews and Arabs together solving the water shortage problem or about an old Jew exhorting a young one to respect all those who dwelled in the land.

In between chapters there were short selections of important and useful information: words that had entered Hebrew from the Latin (*sandlar,* shoemaker, from *sandlarius; tiron,* new recruit, from *tiro; signon,* style, from *signum*); university mottoes with Hebraic roots (Harvard, Yale, Cornell, Dartmouth). Here was the meeting point for the two passionate pursuits of my grandfather's life: the teaching of truly novice students and the study that took place in the highest realms of scholarship.

Tiron, tiro marked the journey between afternoon schools, synagogues, and high schools—the simple, first steps toward proficiency in a new language—all the way to the vast university libraries peopled by erudite professors and eager graduate students. Vocabulary lists, short and quickly mastered, hinted at the thick lexicons that existed elsewhere, the abbreviated codes of etymologies and origins, the secret news for scholars.

הַסֵּפֶר הָעִבְרִי בָּאֲמֶרִיקָה

Hebrew Books and Magazines Published in America

[295]

From *Modern Hebrew*, (1946). The Hebrew Press in America.

Tiro, tiron. The new recruits were to the newest of armies, the Israeli Defense Forces. You could find the beginnings of that language in my grandfather's book. You could find as well listings of the ministries of the Israeli government, places to visit in Israel, important dates in modern as well as ancient Jewish history, and the anthem of the State of Israel and its Declaration of Statehood.

Grandpa Harry's book was everywhere but in my school. My teacher, Etti, had come to Ann Arbor in 1978 from Jerusalem, speaking a fluid, rapid, native Hebrew. She had never heard of my grandfather's Diasporic manual, yet she shared with him the passion for Hebrew and for language in general. Where my grandfather's book was about structures and systems, patterns, syntax, and punctuation, Etti loved words, one after the other—unconnected, small entities of their own; strange and solid as stray objects that had made their way to your hand. While my grandfather's zest for language made him courtly and refined, Etti's made her dissolute and lavish, unteacherly. Each week she ran off a ditto with fifty to one hundred words, sometimes all in lavender print, sometimes in pale green or pink, sometimes all three, miraculously distinct on the paper. The words smelled intensely of the rollers of ink that occasionally needed to be replaced; the sheets were damp and curved, cold to the touch until they dried, the vivid ink fading slightly. From the endless roll of words you could choose any twenty for the weekly dictation test.

The traditional and conventional mixed with the radical in Etti's method. I memorized like a child reciting "See Spot run," but I memorized words like *l'haf'il,* להפעיל, to activate; *menutak,* מנותק, alienated; *mehqar,* מחקר, research; *meratek,* מרתק, fascinating; *adrikhal,* אדריכל, architect; *ukhlusia,* אוכלוסיה, population; *l'hizdahot,* להזדהות, to identify with; *tasbikh elionut* and *tasbikh nehitut,* תסביך עליונות ונחיתות, superiority complex and inferiority complex; *tahburah,* תחבורה, transportation; *hetkeflev,* התקף לב, heart attack; *rashlanut,* רשלנות, negligence; *shtifat mo'ah,* מח שטיפת, brainwash; *liglug,* לגלוג, mockery; *shi'amum,* שעמום, boredom; *ta'alumah,* תעלומה, propaganda; *tovanah,* תובנה, insight; *l'hitalef,* להתעלף, to faint; *limonada,* לימונדה, lemonade.

I learned to say words whose English meanings I could not guess, words that belonged to professions I would never enter. I wrote sentences with the glorious, arcane nouns of specialized locales: the *sh'varim,* שברים, shards, of archaeological sites; *sam'man,* סממן, the flavorful ingredients of tisanes, potions; *bitza, bitzot,* ביצה, ביצות, the bogs of early settlers in Palestine, the source of their malaria and their stories. I misused words, wrenched them from their true, melodic senses. I described the *bitza* of Midwestern puddles in our front yard and evoked *sh'varim* made of paper, a sort of confetti, when *sh'varim* are always ceramic, always sharp and dangerous cracked things.

Each week for a year I inscribed upon my mind twenty new, utterly unrelated, sometimes useless but unfailingly adult words. None would ever appear in an American child's Hebrew book or a student's primer. Few, it seemed to me, would appear in my grandfather's letters, where sentence flowed after sentence and nouns disappeared into metaphor and figures of speech, so that in the end there was little specific to recall. Nothing had happened; nothing had been related, but a fragrance and music filled the room: style, loveliness, elegance, perfection.

The habitual assignment of tired teachers—sentences with spelling words—enchanted me that year of third grade and that year only, for I knew how rare would be the occasions to use words such as *ukhlusia* or *sh'tifat moah* in my daily, even my epistolary, life. I loved Mondays because we got our new lists on that day, and when in fifth grade I had to write a biographical essay in Hebrew, I wrote on Eliezer Ben-Yehuda, the founder of Modern Hebrew and the compiler of its first dictionary.

. . . .

1979

When my Israeli grandparents left Israel and came to live in Ann Arbor, their lift preceded them. Their "lift": a word for transatlantic shipment that I had heard only with reference to Israel. When they arrived to seek the medical care Grandpa Harry needed, my grandmother took control and rebuilt her apartment as an exact replica of the home they had left in Jerusalem.

Like exiled Jews rebuilding their last dwelling place in their new one, Grandma Ann reassembled her shrinelike living room. My grandfather had nothing to do with the living room; I doubt if he could picture it in his dreams. The living room was nothing but the waiting room for the world to come, which was his study.

When Grandpa Harry was busy in his study, I took in the carefully placed mementos on the living room bookshelves. Souvenirs from my grandparents' travel, there were tiny, smiling Mexican figurines in yellow and red sombreros, blue and white china teacups, a set of small Danish wooden clogs, a miniature Westminster Abbey, a silver bell, a box made of shells. *Tchatchkes,* my other grandmother, Birdie, would have said. Good only for looking at, simulacra of past times and places, tourist traps. But Grandma Ann loved them, and each had its place. She dusted them, smiled at them, was eager to tell their histories to her visitors. I never touched them.

Like the souvenirs, the books in the living room were polite literature, almost a kind of furniture for company, though Grandma Ann had read them all. Leather-bound volumes of Browning and Lamb, Fielding and Molière, abutted *Reader's Digest* anthologies labeled *Fun and Laughter, Anecdotes for the Family, Great Stories;* Jewish American writers like Bellow, Potok, I. B. Singer, and Wiesel next to Margaret Mead's *Coming of Age in Samoa* and Lillian Hellman's *An Unfinished Woman.* The oversized *A Dictionary of Quotations* on the very top shelf, next to a volume from the 1950s entitled *Women Are Wonderful; Western Masterpieces of Art* and E. H. Gombrich's studies in art; *Western Masterpieces of Music; Western Masterpieces of Literature.* Pocket dictionaries of French, Spanish, German; a large atlas; histories of the world. Anything a person needed to be literate, my grandmother had. Yet pride of place went to a number of annual volumes of *Who's Who in American Letters, Who's Who in College Education, Me VaMe in Israel,* because Grandpa Harry merited a paragraph in each.

Grandma Ann collected accomplishments. The *Who's Who* volumes yielded to beautifully bound volumes of my grandfather's translations of the medieval philosopher Averroes from Arabic into English and Hebrew. Such volumes, published by the Medieval Academy of America, were the possessions only of scholars or libraries. They stood next to the more popular works of my grandfather's adviser from Harvard, Harry Wolfson, the renowned scholar of philosophy. My grandmother spoke of him in a hushed voice.

The textbooks Grandpa Harry had written, *Ivrit Hayah, Modern Hebrew* and *Sefer HaDikduk V'HaHibur: The Book of Grammar and Composition,* stood next to the academic works, and alongside all these male compositions was my father's tall navy volume, "Flutes: A Study of Periodic Dissolution Profiles Resulting from the Interaction of a Soluble Surface and an Adjacent Turbulent Flow," the dissertation that earned him his Ph.D. from the University of Michigan in 1969.

But this was the living room. In my grandfather's study stood all the really serious volumes, the books he had bought with hard-earned money over the course of his life and marked very lightly and carefully in thin, penciled notations in Hebrew. His name, Tsvi Blumberg, the son of Pinchas, was inscribed on the flyleaf in elegant Hebrew characters, followed often by five Hebrew letters, the definite article *hey,* and then the four letters signifying the Jewish year. This was not a translation of the English date but the year *l'minyan briat ha'olam*, למנין בריאת העולם, according to the Creation of the World. In some of the books, his English name and the secular date appeared too: "Harry Blumberg, 1928." Some of the prices were still visible.

These books were not for show, and they did not have particularly colorful or interesting spines. Almost all were bound in black tape, with the titles chalked in white in my grandfather's hand. My grandfather's volumes moved from place to place. I understood that they were not books you read to consume or finish but books with which you had a private life. Books that traveled miraculously across oceans, kept you company when you were out of place, when your heart was out of rhythm.

. . . .

As many books as my father's parents had, my mother's parents had few. My mother's parents were Birdie and Sam; to Jonathan, Naomi, and me, they were Bubbi and Poppy, and they were New York.

In their home on the Upper East Side of Manhattan, there was one bookcase, and it was in the dark and dusty corner of the living room, forgotten at the side of the Singer sewing machine, which both my grandparents knew how to use. On the bookshelves stood a few Hebrew prayer books, one of which Poppy had received for his service in the U.S. Army during World War II. Then there was a Maxwell House Passover Haggadah; you got it free with the coffee in the supermarket. There was a Haggadah edited by Elie Wiesel and a pocket-sized *Pirkei Avot*, the Ethics of the Fathers; a *Kitzur Shulhan Arukh*, the code of Jewish law abridged for the layperson; and two tractates of the Talmud that appeared to have been my mother's when she was a high school student. Then there was *The Passover Anthology; The Jewish Life Cycle; The Encyclopedia of Biblical Interpretation;* a worn paperback copy of Uris' *Exodus;* Bellow's *Mr. Sammler's Planet; The Tragedy of*

Hamlet; Treasure Island; a variety of Ramaz Dinner Dance ad books; some mysteries; Hemingway, *The Sun Also Rises; At Camp Kee-Tov*, a bright red kids' book; and a boxed set of Mann's *Joseph in Egypt*. Most of these books bore signs of previous ownership, giveaway prices, or mass distribution. These were not books that had been sought after or chosen. For the most part, they were a small, haphazard collection of books that had come my bubbi's way.

Despite the relative dearth of books in her home, Bubbi was an avid reader. She simply did not own the books she read. Like the girls in *All-of-a-Kind-Family*, my bubbi visited the public library regularly and took shining care of the books she borrowed. Just as the make-believe Library Lady—impossibly good, gentle and forgiving, tall and beautiful in her crisp, starched shirtwaist, her long, modest skirt, her chestnut hair piled up into a "chignon" (but you could imagine it down, flowing over her shoulders as she brushed it in the morning and evening)—just as the Library Lady knew Charlotte, Sarah, Henny, Ella, and Gertie, and just as the librarians in Ann Arbor knew me from story hour and regular visits, the librarians in New York knew my bubbi. They thought of her in her absence, putting aside for her new books that they thought she would like or additional books by her favorite authors. She took them home and read them, and when she was done, she slipped out of the house and down the street to the metal return box outside the Seventy-Ninth Street branch.

. . . .

When my father was a boy in Brooklyn, his father spoke to him only in Hebrew. My mother plays Hebrew records for me and reads me stories in Hebrew. In shul, she is the one who helps me pick out the Hebrew letters I have just begun to recognize.

Is Grandpa my mother's father or my father's?

My mother's parents cannot read Hebrew at all. On Passover at the seder, my mother helps her parents find the place in the Haggadah, while Grandpa Harry rests back in his chair, waiting patiently for them to catch up.

But before the seder, when we are cooking, my bubbi makes the gefilte fish from scratch and the chicken soup. The silver pots on the stove are enormous, and everything is boiling. Together Poppy and I make the haroset, and he helps me chop the pieces of nuts and apples into a very fine paste; he holds the bottle of sweet wine as I tip it toward the bowl; he catches my wrist when I have poured enough. Then he grates the bitter herbs and laughs as he does it.

My bubbi hums the whole time we are working. When I am next to her in the kitchen, it is as if I am in shul. When I am in shul without her, I can imagine being next to her. Her lullabies and her Jewish hummings are one and the same.

We work together in the kitchen, and Bubbi asks me if I want a piece of egg matzah to tide me over until the seder. Chicken livers; why don't I like them anymore, she wants to know. She used to feed them to me by hand, put them on my tongue, hot out of the oven.

....

Bubbi was a keeper of letters. In the living room beside the sewing machine was a stack of ancient envelopes bearing penny stamps and multiple unnecessary blotches of black ink: a pen gone wild, an unpracticed writer. During a winter spent in Florida in the 1950s my bubbi's father had written to her—not telephoned—in his laborious English, an entirely phonetic system. "Boidi," he had written for "Birdie." Then "Boyde." Then "Boydele," the loving diminutive.

When she read his letters to her, she did not just absorb the sense of the message; she had her father at her side, as if he were reclining in the moon shape of her ear, whispering to her. Her father was there in the blotches and the missing r's; the struggles of the lips, teeth, and tongue to shape sounds the ear had not heard early enough in life; the immigrant's creative spellings and the will to mail the letter anyway, as it was. It was not a performance; it was a letter.

My bubbi had a typewriter of her own, upon which she composed her letters, including those to us, her grandchildren. Erratic and sticky, this typewriter announced itself with the sloping grade of line after line, sentences taking dives down, then up. She wrote often and easily, not waiting to hear from us, continuing a conversation whose pieces were full of interest, yet unimportant. What mattered was the material letter, paper against the fingers and palms, the combination of typewriting and manual scrawl, a stamp from New York identical to those we bought and used in Ann Arbor: all this the sign of proximity, an extension of our own hands and bodies. Bubbi had held the paper, fed it to her crazy typewriter, watched it come off the roll, folded it, placed it inside the random envelope, stamped and addressed it, brought it to the mailbox. It was her letter, then ours, and when I opened her frequent, quick notes, I knew she was writing because she had thought of us, because she was always thinking of us.

Occasionally, when I opened a letter from her, I would find what she called a "corner" of stamps; that was the special part of the page of stamps you could get at the post office. I imagined her asking for the "corner" the way she asked for our favorite parts of meat at the butcher's. The corner was the collector's item of the stamp sheet because it had a serial number. The problem with the corner, though, was that it seemed to render the stamps unusable. They had a value beyond their use, and so they went inside the envelope as a gift, rather than outside as payment. The corner told the secret of our letters: that they were not what they seemed but a different sort of noncurrent currency; that in the flow of our letters, something was being saved—not the everyday news or the weather, the plans for a visit or the remembrance of one, the request for a special gift or the thanks, but an essence that looked precisely like those things and was nonetheless magical, historical, long-lasting, impossible to calculate.

....

My parents' wedding album was the heaviest book I knew except the dictionary my father had given my mother for her birthday in 1966, the year of their marriage. He had written inside, "For Harriet. A few words and a great deal of love." The Random House volume had no picture on its dull gray cover, but that made it all the more impressive. Since we owned no heirloom books, no prized sets, no first editions, and no encyclopedias; since my parents read often but did not study one text time and again, the dictionary was the book I associated with our family and household. My parents used it occasionally for Scrabble, but more often my father would take it out of its place in order to look up a word someone had used. He liked to tell us what language its root came from and the forms through which it had passed to become the word we knew.

The dictionary held down our house, but it did not interest me as the wedding album did. The album was all images except for the first page, where the invitation to the wedding was superimposed upon the image of my parents. Surface and depth: as if you could magically see through tuxedo and gown to my parents' deepest insides, and what was there were words. Words of invitation, convocation, and consecration.

The text of the invitation belonged to Grandpa Harry, who had perfected the traditional formulation with all the linguistic knowledge he possessed, as if he had gathered it all, from his childhood to late middle age, just for this moment. Then my parents had composed its translation into English. All readers, all invited guests, would open the card to a version they could understand.

When I opened the album to that strange first page of faces and words—a dress and a suit and a veil and a bowtie and also the letters *aleph* and *bet,* all the way to *tav*—the black Hebraic letters jumped like flashing fish on my mother's white dress, matte and dull. My father balanced upon a mat of formal English characters. Black, still, they shone through his black suit, leapt off his well-shined shoes, his parted hair.

This weave, black upon black, white upon white, was something I had never seen before. I could not imagine lifting the invitation out from under my standing parents. I could not imagine depriving the paper of the bodies.

....

The wedding album in our house was one of three: ours, my mother's parents', and my father's parents'. When Jonathan and I pored through the albums on visits to New York and Jerusalem, in our home in Ann Arbor, I worked to find discrepancies, small differences that would say one volume was not the same as the other; the way, when I discovered that in the acrostic prayer of *Ashrei,* the letter *nun* was missing, I wondered if it was so only in my *siddur,* my prayer book and if I might find the missing sentence in another volume.

It intrigued me that books came in copies, that identicality was held out as a promise. Who were the people that made sure of this? Who made sure that the printing machines did not skip a letter, that even if a mistake dotted a page, all such pages would be so dotted, so that "the book" now meant that mistake too?

Books were the opposite of Scrabble: first, the possibility of any word; then, the assembling of words; but finally the scrambling of the letters back in the bag, a return to forgetfulness, which felt at that moment less like possibility than loss.

When I went to the library and saw multiple copies of books, I was both reassured and slightly chagrined. Copies made sure a book would not be lost from the world; if my volume were burned or soaked or simply lost, around the next corner there would be another one. Yet there would not be another one with my name on the inside cover; there would not be another one with my mother's penciled note recording that when I was three, I knew this story by heart; there would not be the page on which my sister Naomi had scribbled when she was too young to have known the difference. That was what would be lost, those differences, insignificant to the story or lesson, song or poem; meaningful only to a specific owner. Precisely the things the library denied you: not owning a book meant not distinguishing it from any other copy. If you wrote inside it, you had to pay for it and it became yours, even if you had not wished it to. They sent you home with it, a gift become a punishment.

In Bubbi's house in New York, a house with relatively few books, there were nonetheless three copies of Grandpa Harry's Hebrew book. They did not stand next to each other on one shelf but were dispersed among other books. The first one was covered with the brown paper of a supermarket bag; my mother told me that before children could keep their own books, school books had gotten covered that way for protection. Its cover and spine were hidden. I knew it was Grandpa Harry's book only because I had opened it, wondering what I would find inside.

The second copy had a stranger's name on the flyleaf, with an old-fashioned New York phone exchange, letters and numbers, penciled in under the name. I wondered if Bubbi had bought it at a rummage sale or found it somewhere, unwanted, and, taking mercy on it and also on its author, whom she knew personally, given it a home.

The third copy was a gift:

June 1966. To our gracious and wonderful
"Mehutanim," Birdie and Sam Garfinkel,
with love and esteem, Harry Blumberg.

Though this copy was clearly the valuable one, my maternal grandparents did not seem to distinguish between it and the two forlorn copies that had belonged first to others, then come to them by chance.

The inscription made all the difference to me. Finally, an heirloom in our family, a marriage gift, an ancient dowry, bag of coins, hope chest. Knowing the difference in values, I wanted the gift book as my own when I discovered it. I was not interested in reading the book or doing its exercises; I was interested in the autographs. Like finding the single prayer book that possessed an alternate *Ashrei*, a long-lost line beginning with the letter *nun*, finding this volume meant I had discovered a secret, one of a kind.

I left it on Bubbi and Poppy's shelves because their home was a home of secrets, of dresser drawers to be pulled open, closets to be rummaged through, and dusty books to be opened. Nothing was in order, which meant that anything might be a treasure. The general stasis of their home begged me to investigate for change each time we arrived to visit. The big, rusty scissors that lay on the bottom shelf of the bookcase had been revealed to me by my poppy as his own father's scissors; with them his father, a tailor, had cut the patterns for my mother's most special baby clothes; with them he had fed his family on the Lower East Side. But the scissors had lain there under cover, and only when I asked had Poppy remembered them there at all.

When I returned the next time—I was eleven now—the scissors were still there. When I reached for my Grandpa Harry's book, though, this time it was not dusty, and when I opened it, its pages were filled with the marks of thick lead pencil in English and Hebrew. My bubbi had filled in the answers to the *targilim la-talmid ha-mathil*, תרגילים לתלמיד המתחיל, the exercises for the beginning student.

....

What I knew about Grandma Ann was that she had been Grandpa's student in a synagogue afternoon school. A well-educated girl makes a better match, her own grandfather had told her. In New York she had sat at her desk and memorized the foreign sounds, read short lessons, participated in spoken dialogues. Her teacher leaped about the room; he brought the language to life; he used the blackboard and the desk, a map and an occasional photograph, and he conjured a land and its syllables. Holidays and Bible stories were part of this study, but they came after modernity. Though they were its roots, they were also its afterthoughts. Zion and Diaspora temporarily reversed themselves too; the center of the world for my grandfather and his students was right there—the unadorned, wondrous classroom.

Grandpa Harry was a teacher from necessity and desire; his own father had died when he was barely a teenager, and he had had no choice but to support the family: three sisters, a brother, and a mother. Out of that necessity he had met his future wife, though she did not know it. To her he was merely and monumentally the teacher. He was the focus of everyone's eyes, and while he looked at them, she was unsure what he saw.

She too would become a teacher, but she taught English, and she taught it to children. In the South Bronx she made children classroom monitors; she helped them sharpen pencils; she gave them the language that their own parents barely had. She lived with her grandparents and her cousin until the day my grandfather called. Ten years had passed; he had come and gone from Harvard University; now he held its diploma and a sturdy wooden chair with its scarlet, gold, and black insignia. Ph.D. in hand, he had something to offer a woman, even in the years of the Depression. He called and said, "Guess who?" She threw over the dentist she was seeing, and three months later she and my grandfather were married.

Two American children raised in immigrant poverty, they went on tour the year of their marriage. Grandpa Harry secured grants for research, and they traveled against the current of history. Through the libraries of Europe, they saw the world, its past and its threatening future. Public squares, fountains, museums, opera houses, cathedrals, crypts, arcades. London, Rome, Vienna, Paris, Munich. At the last, Nazis in uniform scared them, so they cut short their European stay and made precipitously for their final planned leg before returning home.

When they reached Palestine, they entered at the port of Haifa, Grandma Ann's camera in her hand. On film she captured a lone camel, a man in *qaffiyeh*, the walls of the Old City, an Arab festival in Jerusalem, olive trees, sand and sand and sand. They entered the port of Haifa and they left from it, but when they left, my grandmother vowed her return. It was her homeland, she said. My grandfather's language, my grandmother's country. Study brought them there, and it gave them the words to describe it.

In New York in the 1940s and 1950s, they raised my father in Hebrew, Grandpa Harry talking fluidly, Grandma Ann breaking her teeth over it, like the legendary good wife of the ideologue Eliezer Ben-Yehudah. My father and his sister studied Hebrew at home and at their school, a Modern Orthodox yeshiva. The synagogue and school were Orthodox, but the faith of the family was largely secular: a revival of the Jewish people who would work in a land of their own in a once holy tongue made suitable for the everyday. An Orthodox synagogue was simply a Jewish synagogue.

When it came time for my father's Bar-Mitzvah, my father prepared to learn his portion. With the rabbi at school, he learned the melody of the chanting of the Torah, and he put to that melody the oldest words in the language. His portion was *Toldot*, תולדות: these are the generations of Jacob or (according to another translation) these are the stories of Jacob. What is born is what is told; with the child comes the story.

His voice still high, he sang the story of Joseph, the seventeen-year-old who taunted his brothers and wound up exiled to Egypt. From there the history of the Jewish people unfolded: these are the stories, these are the generations. From Jacob to the chariots of Egypt, to the crossing of the Red Sea and then the Jordan, to the prophets who recalled Jacob no longer as the man himself but as a name for all his descendants, the children of Jacob. Jacob, a principle in the world. Jacob, with a name changed to Israel. The one who followed his brother, Esau, who came at his heel, became the one who struggled—*ki sarita*, כי שרית—with God and man and prevailed. From "these are the generations," to the children of Israel, to a land and the prophets who charged a people with misusing the land, defiling its holy places, abusing its spirit.

The story rolls forward, and my father stands at the *bimah*, singing the words his father works from every day. Though his father teaches Hebrew at James Monroe High School—there are not yet any American universities that offer Modern Hebrew as a subject, and he cannot find the rare position in medieval Arabic philosophy—Grandpa Harry will later find his way back to the university: Hunter College of CUNY and later still Tel-Aviv University. There will be time to write articles on bilingual pedagogy but also to turn to the Jewish contemporaries of his Arabic writers. Maimonides and Saadia Gaon, medieval philosophers troubled by the problem of evil in the world: how can God, Who is good, create that which is not good? Time to study and write upon the problem of divine providence and whether it extends beyond the prophet, whether it is particular or general. Also upon the physical characterization of God in the Bible: how do the Jewish philosophers understand the "hand of God," "the form of God," "and God came down," "the eyes of God," "may God shine his face upon you"?

Each of these problems originates in the scroll from which my father reads. Though my grandfather works with books, not scrolls; though his Harvard chair resides in an office and not a Beit Midrash, a house of religious study, still he spends his days with the selfsame holy texts. He prefers to see these texts with a pencil in hand, but on Saturdays, on Shabbat, he hears them read aloud by men who do not study as he does, who do not read with the Sephardic pronunciation of the scholar and the *maskil*, the Enlightenment man.

When he hears the scroll read by the pious, his mind either rests or it rushes through the consequences of the verses, their appearance in later arguments and intellectual episodes. Though my grandfather sits in the synagogue as his father did before him, he knows the recesses of Widener and the British Museum. He and my grandmother have been around the world in service of the scroll on the wooden table at the center of the synagogue. The eternal light shines down on that scroll and on their son's face.

After his Bar-Mitzvah, my father *leyns* (chants) from the Torah regularly. He and a friend from school alternate sabbaths; one week he reads; the next week, his friend. To prepare the reading, they must master the words and match the melody to them, then chant from a scroll that bears no vowels, no punctuation, and no notes, just words barely separated one from the next, words in thick black ink, columns and columns, one indistinguishable from the next unless they can catch a familiar word, a word that locates them, that miraculously transforms the surrounding words and columns into the poetry and prose they recognize, that they have been studying all week in preparation for this public reading. For this task of repetition and performance, my father and his friend are happy to earn five dollars. It is not a small sum. In two years, they have both chanted through the entire Five Books of Moses.

Weekly Grandpa Harry and my father go to the *shtiebel*, the small shul. Women, and not particularly disposed, Grandma Ann and my aunt do not come.

My father hears some of the great cantors of his day; he learns to distinguish between styles of prayer and chanting; he modifies his own rhythms and emphases until he is satisfied with the sound. Though he *leyns* at a small shul in the Bronx, the scroll will be the same anywhere he goes. Though this shul is the one in which he stands, his voice joins with all the other voices the world over reading this week's portion: melodiously, harshly, piously, unthinkingly, for the first time, for the hundredth time. Young voices, old ones, men all over the world announce the words to their congregations. Servants of a sort, princes of a kind, they fulfill the obligation and enable others to do so as well. In doing so, they learn things by heart. They acquire Torah.

....

When I was ten, my father taught me how to leyn. *To* lain, *to* leyn? *I did not know what the word meant, how it was spelled, or where it came from (Yiddish), but I knew how to do it.*

It was new, my father teaching me. My aunt had not learned, nor my mother, certainly not my grandmothers nor any women before them. When they came to the synagogue, they had listened to the male voices whose timbre and tone they expected. They learned their own ages from the high sound of the Bar-Mizvah boy, with his still unchanged voice; the confident young man and father, chanting smoothly; the grunting familiarity of the old man, repeating words of his own three-quarters of a century: anniversaries of Bar-Mitzvah, fifty years of marriage, the birth of a grandchild. It was always a translation, from the man to the woman. Or no translation at all.

"To leyn" *was a specific term, applicable only to chanting the weekly portion from the Torah. It did not have to do with praying, except that the Torah was read during prayer services. It meant affording the community the opportunity to hear its holiest text read flawlessly and melodically.*

My father and I sat together Shabbat afternoons and weekday evenings, and he listened to me read aloud; my brother and sister played happily, knowing they would follow along soon enough. Before music came words. In Hebrew, I learned the value of stressing the right syllable because it might mean the difference between past and present or the difference between a noun and a verb. I knew to note the dot in the letter hey *when it came at the end of a word and to enunciate it with the extra breath that indicated female possession instead of the feminine form of noun, verb, or adjective. Make sure to note when a letter produces a hard sound or a soft sound, my father reminded me; in this case, it is not an issue of meaning but a matter of integrity, respect for detail, respect for the listening community.*

After reading, we sang. Another pattern. Like musical notation, with notes on a staff, the written signs for various notes and melodies floated below and above the words on the page. I learned the names of the recurring melodies first, putting just the names of the notes to song, like the children in The Sound of Music singing "Doe, a deer," to learn the scale. *Once I knew my scale, meaningful words replaced the nonsense names of notes. Sentences came, first with difficulty, then more naturally. I repeated them aloud until I knew them by heart: dialogue, drama, phrases and chapters that I could not understand yet but that I acquired nonetheless. Walking around with language that waited for me around corners of time and place, impossible to anticipate or rush, I hosted the thing that hosted me.*

. . . .

1980

Of the books in my mother's parents' home, the most well-worn was the *siddur*, the Birnbaum prayer book. Like my parents' wedding invitation, the text was Hebrew on one side and an English translation on the other. Each Wednesday morning, Bubbi took the Lexington Avenue bus to her synagogue, her *siddur* under her arm, for the class in Synagogue Hebrew. Like Grandpa Harry, the scholar, she too penciled notes in her text, but her notes were not the notes of the assured mind, the confident, almost hubristic, questions that the practiced reader poses in the margins of a speechless text.

My bubbi took the notes of a humble student. In capital letters she wrote in the English pronunciation of Hebrew words, a transliterating code that was meant to gain her access to the rituals and the world of Saturday morning. Each week she went to synagogue. Rain or shine, she put on a dress and applied some lipstick, tucked soft tissues into her old purse, and walked the eight blocks and three avenues to her synagogue; Poppy accompanied her only rarely. Like my other grandparents, Bubbi and Poppy were non-Orthodox members of an Orthodox synagogue. Yet what a difference for the shul-goer to be the woman, not the man!

Each week my bubbi sat in the same seat. Each week, alone, she gazed down from the vaulted balcony at the miniature rabbi and the white men all around him. Her joy was like my own before a doll house, perfectly arranged.

She saw the velvet, the tall Ark, the rabbi's top hat, the soft fringes of the *talleisim* (prayer shawls), the table upon which the Torah was read and the aisles down which it was carried; the silver bells and crowns; the slow, definite melodies, repeating weekly; the camaraderie among the men and its translation among the wives and daughters; the immense rose window, rising high above, as if it were the sky and everything underneath were sedentary, earthly.

Each week she followed the foreign language with her finger, often finding herself a few words behind, having to skip forward until her eyes could match enunciated sound to the most common words, familiar as signposts: *kadosh*, holy; *barukh*, blessed; *yisrael*, Israel; *melekh*, king.

The idea of having a conversation in Hebrew did not captivate her. The whole idea behind Grandpa Harry's book was not her plan. She did not desire to go shopping in Hebrew or order a sandwich or decipher a weather report. She did not long to hear the keening notes of Yehudah Ha-Levi, mourning for Jerusalem, unable to taste the pleasure of anything upon his tongue while living in exile. And she did not appreciate my grandfather's modernized, secularized versions of biblical and Talmudic tales—Abraham without God, Sinai without law, Akiva without yeshiva. She had little taste for what was new and nationalistic, political, or artistic; she needed what was old, trustworthy, and mystical.

My bubbi's laborious language had given unnatural birth to a daughter whose language could be swift and easy. In the school Bubbi had chosen for her—the same yeshiva day school my father's parents had chosen for him—my mother came to know the Hebrew alphabet as she knew the English. She learned songs, prayers, plays, rhymes, stories, dances, and jokes; she read Hebrew without a thought of how its sounds might look transliterated into English. She read the Hebrew of a new state and the Hebrew of an ancient people without thinking much about it. Synagogue Hebrew was the easiest of all. In a singsong and a chant and rollicking melodies, the children—not yet Bar-Mitzvah, not yet men and women divided into balcony and floor, actors and audience—memorized every prayer. It became almost impossible to think of the meaning of the words or to think of the ideas of difficulty or choice or intention. The song buoyed them, as it was meant to.

In school my mother's class took a field trip to the synagogue. There the children saw the Torahs close up. They could see that the paper was not paper at all but the fantastic dried skin of an animal and that the ink was like no ink they had ever used but something indelible, staining, immutable, and austere. The letters were made of feathers and sticks and bones that became crowns and pinnacles and thrones and palaces. The *atzei hayim* of the Torah, its wooden handles, were soft to the touch, smoothed by years of handling. Anonymous hands, honored hands. The silver was bright, not needing any polish. My mother had never seen silver so bright. And the filigree in the finger of the pointer, the tool with which those who read from the Torah kept their place, was fine and cool, like a locked gate.

It was not until the occasion of my mother's wedding, however, that my bubbi found herself in the home that she had glanced down into and desired for so long. There, in the deep, almost underground space from which rose up the formulaic, incantatory words *kadosh, barukh, yisrael, melekh,* קדוש, ברוך, ישראל, מלך. Bubbi and Poppy escorted my mother, a veiled bride, down the central aisle of the synagogue.

Suddenly there they stood—the two women—at the center, at the red, velvet heart of the Jewish world, where all the men stood. Where those who knew stood. Where the Torahs stood and where the great mystery of the Hebrew letters began.

My bubbi never stood there again, nor did my mother.

I have looked down into that space from above but never stood inside it. Praying at my bubbi's side, I have imagined jumping or falling over the railing of the balcony, wondering what a falling female body might look like from above, from below, surprised that no girl has yet had the courage or the decency or the fear to fall.

I have imagined a twirling female body, whirling through air and across time, flying past the rose window, swinging past the white velvet curtain covering the Ark, brushing against the red velvet that is spread over every other surface as if to keep away the evil eye, to keep out the city sounds, to keep the peace and to absorb all the echoes and perhaps even blood.

. . . .

1982

Yet across the country, in the Midwest of America, I, the daughter and granddaughter, a girl and young adult, stood at my father's side, among men and women, and chanted aloud from the Torah as my father had taught me. We prayed in a Conservative synagogue since now if you were not thoroughly Orthodox, you had a choice. If you had daughters, you had a choice.

Though my mother did not approach the Torah, I saw the inside of the Torah opened to more than one portion. It was my daily life; it was what one did; it was being a Jew and a daughter. I sang unconscious of the blackness of the print and the dryness of the parchment. The silver may have been tarnished, and the cloth may have been frayed. None of this mattered because I was after a sound and a rhythm.

Standing on the *bimah,* I ran after the words that were always ahead of me, always already there, having beaten me to the finish. I tried to catch up, to reach the ending—Mount Nevo, Moses looking over the land, having blessed all his sons and tribes: *v'shamah, lo ta'avor,* ושמה לא תעבר: I have shown it to you in sight, but in body, you shall not cross over—but I never reached that verse. Always, I was reading from the middle, whether the scroll was rolled heavily on one side or the other; I read from the middle of the scroll, a young girl, not fit for the end of a *sefer,* the crashing finales of human history.

First, I read Egypt: until when will these people be a thorn in our sides, send them out, send them out. I read Pharoah's manipulated resistance and his quick capitulation.

I read the buying of a burial plot for a wife once barren.

I read Isaac's famine and later his hunger for a delicacy before death; then I read a chosen son dressed in animal skins before a blind father once sacrificed like a beast upon an altar.

Joseph preened before his brothers; he lost his coat; his father saw it bloody; the wife of Moses circumcised her own son with a rock, making him a bridegroom of blood.

A people danced among molten gold; God refused to erase his hero from his story; then the hero pleaded with God, using against Him His own name: the threat of a slanderous story.

Tablets, spies, watermelons and garlic, meat and manna, houses that contracted leprosy, vessels and garments too. The rising of the sun, the counting of days, dipping in collected waters, purity at sunset.

"If you hearken to my voice...."

"If you don't...."

"The good of the land...."

"And you shall sow in vain. . . ."

Kotz v'dardar, קוץ ודרדר, thorns and thistles;

"The voice of your brother's blood calls out to me from the earth";

"Erase me from Your book";

"My father, do you have but one blessing?"

V'shamah lo ta'avor, ושמה לא תעבר: but there, you shall not arrive.

Eved hashem, עבד ה': the servant of God.

L'eynei kol yisrael, לעיני כל ישראל: before the eyes of all Israel.

If They Be Two

A Valediction: Forbidding Mourning

As virtuous men pass mildly away,
And whisper to their souls to go,
Whilst some of their sad friends do say
The breath goes now, and some say, No;

So let us melt, and make no noise,
No tear-floods, nor sigh-tempests move;
'Twere profanation of our joys
To tell the laity our love.

Moving of th'earth brings harms and fears,
Men reckon what it did and meant;
But trepidation of the spheres,
Though greater far, is innocent.

Dull sublunary lovers' love
(Whose soul is sense) cannot admit
Absence, because it doth remove
Those things which elemented it.

But we by a love so much refined
That our selves know not what it is,
Inter-assurèd of the mind,
Care less, eyes, lips, and hands to miss.

Our two souls therefore, which are one,
Though I must go, endure not yet
A breach but an expansion,
Like gold to airy thinness beat.

If they be two, they are two so
As stiff twin compasses are two;
Thy soul, the fixed foot, makes no show
To move, but doth, if th' other do.

And though it in the center sit,
Yet when the other far doth roam,
It leans and herkens after it,
And grows erect, as that comes home.

Such wilt thou be to me, who must,
Like th'other foot, obliquely run;
Thy firmness makes my circle just,
And makes me end where I begun.

—JOHN DONNE (1633)

Philadelphia, 1997

From the time I was a child I knew books were objects as well as voices. Things of which I was momentarily master, I took them off my bookshelves and laid them on the floor. I covered the carpet with them. They would all return to shelves (how would I walk otherwise?), but when they did, they would possess a new order and new identities. One week I would organize according to alphabetical order; another week, by genre. I learned to shelve by topic, as the Dewey decimal system did; then I moved to publisher. I liked the strange mix of sense and nonsense in shelving by publisher: the stretch of books all the same height and width, you could run your hand over their flat tops, yet inside the books nothing was alike.

I came to know my books by reading them but also by asking where they belonged. How different a book could seem when it rested between new volumes! I wanted to see my books in all possible lights. I also loved to touch them. I felt a slight consternation laying them on the floor because my mother had already taught me that when you dropped a *siddur*, a prayer book, or a Humash, a Bible, you kissed it upon picking it up. Books did not belong on the floor.

A childhood habit can die hard. Still today, twenty or so years later, I sort my books with love and longing and some anxiety. But I sort out of necessity, not election. I sort when it is once again time to move, when the cardboard boxes have come out and the moving truck has been rented, a new address and apartment found. I am a graduate student in literature at the end of the twentieth century. At twenty-seven, I have moved more times over the years since I graduated college than my grandparents over the course of their entire lives.

The books most precious to me right now are the novels of George Eliot. My edition of *Middlemarch* is the Bantam Classic paperback. The familiar rooster insignia tops the spine upon which the title, author, price ($5.95), and publisher appear. The cover is brick red, inset with the portrait of a woman standing up from her table. Her hands are on her corseted sides while her fingers reach to meet at the small of her back. She leans away from the table, arching her body luxuriously, perhaps painfully. The image of Christian angels in stained glass meets her eye. When I slide the book between its neighbors, the deep color of gems stays with me, an afterimage.

Across the room from George Eliot, Jane Austen, the Brontë sisters, Dickens, Collins, and Trollope, another bookcase stands. Here the books open from right to left. Here the books are hardcover rather than paperback, and their spines are inscribed with gold lettering. Pages are marbled, though many cheaply. This collection begins with the twenty-four books of the Hebrew Bible in an edition called Mikraot Gedolot. Each folio features not only the biblical text, but also major commentaries: the medieval greats, Rashi and Ramban, Ibn Ezra and Sforno. These are scholars who elucidate questions of grammar, literary sense, theological meaning, and human experience. Tall, heavy volumes consisting purely of commentaries on those primary commentaries come next on the shelves.

Then a shelf for tractates of the Mishnah, the earliest codification of Jewish law, compiled by Rabbi Yehudah Ha-Nasi at the close of the second century of the Common Era. Then the entire Talmud, though in a portable set of five thick volumes rather than the massive tens of volumes men have traditionally been given upon marriage. My shelves bear Midrashic discourses, legends, homilies, and sermons; texts of medieval Jewish philosophy and legal codes designed to abstract the law from the long Talmudic discussion in which it originates; eighteenth- and nineteenth-century discourses on purity, holiness, how to walk the path of God and not stray; twentieth-century works on the literary interest of the Bible, on Zionism and religion, on the laws of Shabbat in a technological era, on the role of women in Judaism. From ancient life through modernity, everything is described.

My holy books are never written in. Most are weighty, with sharp corners and relatively taut spines, except the one-volume Humash, or Five Books of Moses, which I have been using since ninth grade. Its binding is taped and double-taped to keep it together. With holy books the loss of a page is more than unfortunate or aggravating. According to Jewish law, holy pages must be buried in the ground, the way one would bury a beloved body.

The laws governing the use of holy books are many and fascinating. You may not rest a book on the same level at which you are sitting—for example, next to you on a bench. If you are studying and get up to take a break for a short while, you must close your book since leaving it open and unattended is a sign of disrespect.

You never place any book on top of the Bible; there is a whole hierarchy, based partly in historical primacy and partly in the attributed divinity of authorship. The *Torah She'be'al Peh,* or the Oral Torah, the Mishnah and Gemara, which together make up the Talmud, are traditionally believed to have been given to Moses on Mount Sinai along with the Written Torah, the first Five Books. However, the rabbis who later recorded the Oral Torah were not prophets of the same stature of Moses. All this is to say that the Talmud goes underneath the Bible in the pile of books on your desk or table, and the work of the Rambam, a central medieval philosopher and codifier of law, goes underneath the Talmud.

Frequently if you open a holy book in the library of an individual, in a school, a synagogue, or a yeshiva, you will find three letters inscribed where you might expect to see a name, a declaration of ownership: *lamed, hey, vav.* The acronym stands for לה׳ הארץ ומלאה, *La'shem ha'aretz u'mloah:* to God belongs the earth and all that fills it. The practical import of this verse, appearing here inside the book, is to say, go ahead, use this book with the owner's blessing. Sometimes, in smaller letters, underneath the authorization, whose quasi-legal purpose is to affirm the act of reading as an innocent one and dismiss any resemblance to theft, you may see the phrase *B'hezkat X:* in the temporary possession of X, the owner's name.

I have always been moved by this combination: the desire to share, to abdicate privacy, possession, and definition in favor of community and generous circulation, and then at the very same time the impulse to affirm that it matters deeply what each one of us owns in this earthly world. Doors shut upon houses, and in the dark, by the light of a lamp (or once, a candle), our books are home, and they make our walls.

....

We read together almost every night. We sit in his house, his one room facing the street, while against the sky, the unlikely Russian-looking spires rise up from the tops of houses in greens, yellows, and reds from night into morning. Reading is different at night and in the morning. At night the room is dark, its two corners brightly lit. The phone does not ring; there are no interruptions. From the street three floors down, only the barest echo of sound reaches us. None of my friends or family knows where I am or how to reach me. And our friends from graduate school leave us in privacy.

In the silence I lie curled up in the green chair, and my legs lean on the soft corduroy footrest. I am in the sort of clothes that say night is here til morning; there is no going anyplace now. Home and the day is done. John lies on the couch, his head propped up by a pillow from the bed, his feet bare, his Oklahoman cowboy boots resting on the floor by the coffee table. I hold my book, and he holds his.

In morning, the sun pushes in through the dirty windows. In summer it is not yet hot; in winter it is freezing. Half the year, we reach for the fan; the other half, one of us runs to turn on the heat, then comes back to bed. Slowly, we make our way to language and

the new day. We drink coffee, sipping it slowly. I take milk; he drinks it black. Already, books are before us. Waiting. We let them wait. Often, we read together. Often, aloud. Faulkner, Dickinson, Joyce, James, Donne. We read to each other. When John reads, he reads loudly, not in his speaking voice; his voice sounds breathless to me, as if he is made nervous before words he is only borrowing. He always touches me when he reads, and I feel the pulse of the prose or poem in his fingers, tightening and loosening on my knee, my arm. When I read, I read softly but enunciate each word. I wonder what he hears when I read because often when he reads, I am not listening for anything but him.
....

From very early on, it was the stories of lives that I loved. Realist novels and biographies shared the same conventions: birth, growth, adolescence, adulthood, death; conflict, love, passion, vocation; the invisible working of historical conditions on personal destiny. Moving into the world of the characters I met, I learned the readerly sympathy that would serve me well when, at nineteen, I encountered the novels of George Eliot, which I would study for years to come.

Distinctive as she was, George Eliot followed perfectly on the heels of all my childhood reading. By the time I reached *The Mill on the Floss,* I had lived so many lives in reading that the hallmark of her novelistic vision—her directions to adopt not just one but many personalities, to see the story through as many sets of eyes as possible—seemed natural. And the powerful authority of her narrator was an authority I had already bowed to, for years and years, a submission I had learned and desired in the reading of almost every novel. It was the submission to someone else's story, the agreement to put oneself into their hands, to let them take however much time they needed to set the scene, to build suspense, to foster care, to indulge suffering, then to provide comfort, to resolve.

To resolve. Long before I could explain why, I loved the critical hour reached when I had far more pages behind me than ahead, when the book was so heavily weighted toward the left that it would simply close of itself if my hands did not hold it to its promises.

The closer I came to the end, the more nearly was I united with the novel's true hero, its writer. As much as I enjoyed beginnings, setting out in faith, I knew faith was also a form of ignorance. In those early pages, book weighted toward the right, I felt keenly my difference from narrator and novelist. Freed from the trial of construing events without first knowing their ending, the omniscient, omnipotent, flying narrator overcame the medium of living to write the novel. The novel: its tight, beautiful, intricate coherences; its echoes and foreshadowings; its subtle essences streaming subterranean, erupting into full sense only at the end or in the moment of rereading, when the loving, admiring reader put her palm to her forehead in the privacy of the solitary pursuit of her reading and exclaimed with deepening gratitude and wonder, "Now I see. *Now* I see."

Literature for me meant this burst of knowledge. A kind of sight, always slightly belated but immediately appended and incorporated. The next time you would see better, more quickly, more closely. The next time it might not take retrospect or rereading; you would see with the sight of the already dead, the swallow, the wise man, the omniscient narrator.

....

I learned to read the words of the Bible before I learned to read George Eliot, and I began with *aleph, bet,* the first two letters of the Hebrew alphabet. According to the custom of the youngest children's schools in East European shtetls, on our first day of school we too were given large, white sugar cookies, dipped in honey, in the shape of the letters. To sweeten the path of learning. To instruct our mouths, our bodies, in the solidity and ingestability of Torah. To show us as children that Torah satisfies hunger, strengthens the body, and delights the senses.

When in third grade we receive our first Humashim, the slim navy volumes of Genesis, our parents get together in secret before the ceremony to make us bookmarks. I think it is my mother's idea. They have taken two blue lucite sheets, cut them to the size of bookmarks, and, between the sheets, inserted the cut-out shape of a tree. The trunk of the tree is made from beautiful white paper—you can see its grains through the blue transparency—and the tree's crown is made of a shiny gold material, like the crown of the Torah scroll in synagogue rather than the crown of a wholly organic tree. On one side of the white trunk, vertically, each set of parents has written in thin black marker their child's Hebrew name: אילנה, Ilana: *aleph, yod, lamed, nun, hey.* On the other side, they have printed —my mother in her fine, clear Hebrew print—עץ חיים היא, *Etz hayim hi:* it is a tree of life.

Torah, I learn over the years, is a tree. It is water, it is a plaything, it is a well, it is a marriage gift, it is a flame, it is fruit. And it *is* all these things to me. I learn to read it; I learn to read its interpreters, beginning with the medieval commentary of Rashi. Rashi, we learn as children, did not have enough paper or ink; thus his comments are as spare as his materials were scarce. He writes only answers to the questions that haunt his commentary in their absence. Often, to allude to the fact that there is a question, though he has not specified its nature, he will simply say: "This verse cries out, 'Interpret me' ": אין המקרא הזה אומר אלא דרשני.

Over the years that I study Torah I learn to turn to Rashi only when I can foretell what will merit his attention; in this way I start to become an expert on the verses myself. I listen for the mute call of the silences or seeming aberrations of the text. "And Cain said to his brother Abel, and it came to pass when they were in the field and Cain arose against Abel his brother, and killed him." Even as a child, I can guess where Rashi will stop, what will trouble him, though I cannot guess his answer. Rashi will ask, "What is it that Cain said?" "And Cain said to his brother Abel, and it came to pass. . . ." Something crucial is missing. I know whatever he said had to have been hostile or provoking, something that could lead to murder, because that is the consequence of the speech. Rashi may give me an answer, but it is my job first to understand the question.

I learn to read with an eye for mystery, never to skim, never to leap or skip over words or verses. Why do we labor this way? The very premise of our study is that the Torah is intended for us, that its encoded messages were and are God's greatest gift to the Jewish people. "Turn it, and turn it," say the Sages, "for it holds everything": הפך בה והפך בה דכלה בה. Attend to the text with all the care you possess because every difference, every strangeness, every omission, every contradiction, even every convention, calls, "*Darsheini*," "Interpret me."

Of course, there are many ways *lidrosh*, to extract meaning. My tendency was not literal or prescriptive—for instance, deriving from Abraham, who got up in the heat of day and rushed to meet his guests, that one must be a welcoming host. With the characters of the Bible there was no easy identification. In their world wandering men turned out to be angels, women gave birth at one hundred years of age, fathers were told by God to sacrifice sons they had been promised by the very same God.

My imagination was caught up instead by the short, dramatic, memorable phrases. Before I understood their intricate, suggestive meanings, I knew them by heart from the sort of study we did in school. From fifth grade on, my study took place in Chicago at a Solomon Schechter school. My family had moved from Ann Arbor, where the community was too small to sustain a Jewish day school beyond fifth grade. In junior high in Chicago we learned in traditional ways, as valuable to me as they were old. About each chapter, each story, we learned to answer: who said what to whom and in reference to what? We filled in the blanks. We put the verses in order. We memorized and recited. Music helped since my father had taught me to chant from the Torah according to the notes of cantillation followed in the synagogue. From study in school and from chanting them at home I memorized long sections. At times even today I find myself walking the streets singing from memory Sarah's laughter, Hagar's exile, Isaac's binding, Rebecca's deception, Jacob's labor, Rachel's jealousy, Joseph's dreams, Pharaoh's degradation, the people of Israel's entry into the land of Canaan.

But the mastery of the Bat-Mitzvah girl was just the beginning of an arduous path of study. This was why my parents had moved us to Chicago: for us to see just how much there was to learn, to see that just as a secular education broken off at fifth grade would be hopelessly elementary, so too would a Jewish education cut off before adulthood.

In 1984 Chicago offered one coed Jewish high school, an Orthodox one. When I began school there, it became clear that to "learn" beyond the most basic plot, one had to know grammar. We began with the three-letter roots that constitute the basis of most words in Hebrew. From there, we learned to conjugate in present tense, then to add the suffixes of past tense, the prefixes of future, the possessive endings. We mastered masculine and feminine nouns and adjectives, making sure to retain the consistency of plural and singular. By the time we were done, we had been taught five tenses along six paradigms for verbs: continuous action, habitual action, passive, active, interactive, intensified. We knew how to conjugate prepositions as well as nouns, even the exceptions. And those with an ear for the language knew the order in which these words would appear, could guess before seeing the verse how it might read, though one could never guess its poetry.

There was nothing arcane about our knowledge. As soon as it was learned, we applied it to the end of construing Biblical verse. The stakes were high. If you mistake one tense for another, a promise turns to a history, a command to a summary. An active verb or a passive must be read as such; it is not just a matter of grammar, but of identity and power: who acts, who is acted upon. If the meaning of the verb used in one place is ambiguous, your task is to locate another instance in which meaning promises to be more clear. Perhaps then, with the verses side by side, the clear meaning appears suddenly more complicated, while the opaque meaning, you begin to see, bears a very particular meaning you had not anticipated.

This intellectual labor was a great pleasure for me, but it was also an expression of religious faith. The giving of time to study bespoke a belief in the worth of the book and its Author. As scientific and academic as such study was, I was guided by the belief that the outcome of all my linguistic work would be insight. To me the statement of the Sages—"If you have given much time to the study of Torah, do not praise yourself. Because it was for this that you were created"—did not mean only that we were created to study Torah, but that studying Torah would help us know why else we were created.

If we studied, we might come to see what in this world was truly important and what was trivial, what was expected of us and how we might best give it. From devoting ourselves to uncovering the implicit meanings of the text, analyzing both stories and the legal sections of the Bible until we had articulated their most extrapolated, abstract, yet always practical meanings, we might come to see how God saw the world.

....

A banner was hanging on Butler Library, the massive, regal home of Columbia University's books, the year I began my college studies. SAPPHO, red letters cried across the beautiful, wide white banner. BEHN, WOLLSTONECRAFT, AUSTEN, DICKINSON, WOOLF. From photographs I knew that the library was engraved with other names: HOMER, HERODOTUS, SOPHOCLES, PLATO, ARISTOTLE. Yet in my first year at Barnard, the angels guarding passage were these untraditional ones. Clearly they had guarded the passage of the fearless student who had crept undiscovered to the top of the building late at night and hung her flag.

I learned all those female names in my English classes that year. The fragments of Sappho's poetry, women with bodies, blood and moons, longing; Aphra Behn, the first woman to make her living by the pen, her bawdy plays and crafty apologies; Mary Wollstonecraft's *Vindication,* a heady response to Locke, and her didactic fiction calling for women's education and a new philosophy of motherhood; Jane Austen, her satires of courting and marriage and men and women, her parlor world with the shadows of war and empire hovering; and Woolf, blessed Woolf, the mother of feminists: women need good food, they need money, they need space in order to create, to write and excel.

I saw the banner on my way to class but also on my way to pray and *lern,* to study the classical texts of my tradition. In cool, damp morning I crossed Broadway and walked alone down the silent paths of campus. The sleep of students weighted and softened the ground upon which I walked; it was like walking on pillows, in dream and sleep. Yet when I arrived at Earl Hall, other students were awake too, facing day like the miniature adults of the early American paintings I learned about in class: paintings of children before the category had been invented.

Our collective destination was the Beit Midrash, the hall of religious study. There the world of the university faded. The small library of holy texts superseded the stacks of Butler Library. Two tables, a bunch of chairs, two windows, some heat in the winter, a fan in the summer, two narrow bookcases of volumes contributed by the students themselves, left as a legacy for those who would follow. Thus was a small meeting room transformed into a permanent house of study. In an unusual dispensation, the room did not have to be shared with any other university group because we had explained to the officials that there could be no set hours in which we would agree as a community to abandon the Beit Midrash. "And you shall speak these words night and day." There was no rest to Torah study.

The Beit Midrash was home to women and men, yet the content of our study was generally different. With the exception of my friends—nicknamed "the Brovender's girls" after the yeshiva where we had studied in Israel—most women did not study Talmud but Bible or Jewish law or even philosophy; most men studied the Talmud. Carrying the large, manly volumes of Gemara, the Brovender's girls were a colony of discovered Yentls. From our first day in Jerusalem we had learned the value of a good defense. Studying in what was then the only women's institute that focused its energies upon Talmud, a text historically closed to women, we became experts in the arguments for teaching women the Oral Torah. The butt of the university Purim spiels, the Brovender's girls were bright, Ivy League–bound girls. We could learn a page of Gemara as well as any guy, and we were not content to learn among ourselves alone; we wanted men as our study partners. The men we were looking for would be looking for us too: a wife they could learn with and talk to, not relegate to the kitchen and bedroom to bake challah and bear children. We would graduate summa; pursue true careers; meet without fail to study Talmud, not Bible, the old-fashioned women's choice; pray each day in the correct hour, abandoning female license for voluntary obligation. We would also raise children, prepare the meals and house for Shabbat each week, and chair social action committees for our synagogues. The fact that not one of us knew a single older woman who embodied this ideal of achievement did not deter us.

The difficult contradictions of being religious suffragettes found expression in our dress as well as in our minds. Unlike "the skirts"—girls who had attended traditional seminary and covered their knees and elbows with loose clothing—we coveted other things. Yet unlike the girls who had left a lifetime of Jewish schooling with the eager embrace of new college freedoms—miniskirts, tight T-shirts, shorts, flip-flops—we wanted respectability: to respect and be respected.

We were as resourceful within a limited closet as our foremothers had been in their constrained kitchens. From years of dressing experience we had our equivalents for jeans and sweatpants. We had the skirts that bordered on sex and the skirts that were simply comfortable and pleasant to look at. The long, flowy skirts, the short, fitted skirts. The jean skirt. The jean skirt with tights and loafers, the jean skirt with Keds and short socks. The jumper, the casual dress.

Still for all this acquired skill, the archetypal Brovender's girl was the girl with the Gemara, but in pants. Or, even more often, debating the subject of pants. It was our invariable conversation. Trained as fervid students, we naturally gravitated toward the insoluble puzzle, the one that could regenerate itself ceaselessly, daily, yearly. We knew better than any advertiser, any designer, the messages of clothing. The company we called for, the lives left behind, chosen, celebrated by fabric, cut, weave, width. Supposing, we would say, that we found the men who could tolerate—nay, appreciate—the New Women we were, what would happen beyond marriage?

The problem of the skirt yielded immediately to the even more personal problem of the head, the hair. Would we, when we got married, cover our hair in modesty, as the more traditional Orthodox women did? We rehearsed these debates often and in prolonged form because they were our way of asking whether our souls belonged to Orthodoxy or modernity. In talking about skirts and pants and wigs and hats, we were trying out possible futures. Which romance would we construct for ourselves, dress for, try to find? The marriage in which one covered one's hair would be the marriage of quiet, private passion, a passion no one else could know but only guess at. The inside of one's home would be the only inside. Every other place, every other man, would be a place and person who were not home and never could be. If you covered your hair, you were a woman before you were a person. You asked people to look at you and think of your being a woman, think of your sex, and how they could not have it. You were untouchable and unknowable; you held yourself upright, never forgot yourself. That was what covering your hair was meant to ensure: memory of self, memory of what is not self.

Not covering your hair was the American thing to do: the free, magazine-ad look of woman as a person traveling in the world, usually alone, though whatever intimacy she found would be as unabashed and natural as her walk and talk. Not covering your hair was the romance of knowability: you might know others, and they might know you. No one would hesitate before talking to you or approaching you: you were friendly, available, like other people. You belonged to no one but the world; your husband was not destined for you but chosen. Your children were not given to you as a blessing, as a grace, but came naturally, just as all your words to them did, just as your decisions did. No one watches you, and you do not watch yourself.

The fantasy of being the woman with her head covered posed for me a great dilemma. Even as I could imagine such a marriage, could imagine such a husband and such a life (in Israel), I knew that I was redeeming bad merchandise. I knew I should not want to cover my hair; I knew I should be on the side of the women who fought against it, but when I saw my future, I could not help but see hats and scarves. Like a little girl imagining herself grown up yet unable to imagine the transformed face and body that would be hers, I did not imagine myself dressed as a wife and mother because it would not be I. It would be some woman who had given birth to the me that lived now, a woman older and wiser. How could I argue with her?

But these were the secret thoughts. My friends and I spoke of justice, not romance; large social forms, not the strange, mutating shapes of desire. And in the face of the injustices we confronted, we were right to avoid the confusions of desire. First, there was our thorough exclusion from leadership in all prayer services, our uncounted presence absorbing the echo of the voice that traveled toward us, blessing God for having made him a man and not a woman. There were visits home to my family's synagogue in Chicago, where I heard all my male friends called to the Torah. I watched them return to their seats, greeted with warm handshakes by all the men they passed; then two men turned to reprimand me because I had, from my seat at the back of the sanctuary, reached over the *mehitza* for a volume of the commentary I was studying. There were no books on the women's side, I explained.

And there was the ongoing, still passionate debate among Columbia students over women's study of Talmud—for example, what to make of Rabbi Eliezer's statement in the Mishnah that the father who teaches his daughter the Oral Torah has taught her nothing but "licentiousness." Licentiousness.

Across the world from our mentors in Israel, my friends and I invoked their ideas. We reminded ourselves of the passionate professor of Jewish thought (head covered) who had turned to the Gemara to support her claim that it was the practice of people known to be pious that ultimately became validated and confirmed as *halakha,* Jewish law. "If you want to know the law, go look in the market": this was what the rabbis of the Talmud had said in a period of devotion to the law. People devoted to the law did not destroy it. If they altered it slightly or even dramatically, they altered it for the sake of survival or the greatness of God's name.

In practical terms this meant to us that if we were beyond reproach when it came to prayer and study, generosity of behavior, and strictness of law, then our other choices would gain acceptance too. If we were blameless, if we were known to be acting for the sake of heaven, *l'shem shamayim,* then the *halakha* would have to follow in our footsteps.

We took this idea to live by, yet it was not easy. How long would it take, what would we have to sacrifice to prove that we were acting *l'shem shamayim?* All our personal observance of daily prayer and regular study did not suffice. The dictated sexual abstinence did not suffice. Our visible pain at the suggestion that took the Columbia community by storm—that women and men not only pray separately but have separate hours to learn in the Beit Midrash—did not stand for us. Sorrow at the backward step of segregating men and women in the one space that should have existed above law—learning; the utopian instant in which men and women might for once lose the sex and the difference that tinged all other things and put our minds to work in the service of something that was neither one of us, but divine, a text before whom we stood as equals. That sorrow did not prove us either.

I could not understand how the pain of these arguments and our embattled positions did not sufficiently, even amply, prove that we were acting for the sake of heaven, that we were not simply serving our own desires and passions. Why could the powerful rabbis and legislators of our communities not see that if we were not well intentioned, we would have dropped out long ago, with the first frustration, the first affront to dignity, instead of redoubling our efforts? Was it not easier *not* to wake up every morning at six to meet the cold air to go to pray in the quorum of ten men that constituted a public, when the reward for our piety was to be told face to face by the more sympathetic rabbinic authorities that even ten thousand women could never constitute a public?

At this time I believed with firm and whole faith that as harsh and unkind as the rabbis were, God was sympathetic. I spoke to the God in Whom I believed, in a kind of prayer that had come to resemble my communal life. Pleasure and pain were made of the same substance. As the waves of the Red Sea had been blown by wind to solidity, then stood quivering, masquerading as walls, pleasure was unstable, could collapse at any moment into the despair that flowed over the heads of the Egyptians. Or perhaps the flow of water was the pleasure and the walls the pain. I could not tell. When the walls held, I prayed, and after they fell, I prayed from underneath them.

Yet even when one prays intensely, one lives in space, always particular space. Each morning as I would walk to prayer services along the silent paths of the deserted, early morning campus, I nodded to SAPPHO, BEHN, WOLLSTONECRAFT, AUSTEN, ELIOT, DICKINSON, WOOLF. I walked by the banner on my way to pray and learn; then I walked by it later on my way to class. I went to class in skirts, as I had for four years in Orthodox high school and one year in yeshiva. Day after day I had done what I could with a skirt that covered the knees.

But unlike hats and scarves, there were no fantasies associated with skirt wearing. I did not have to teach myself its oppressive nature because I felt it. The abundance of material depressed me. Length, folds, and pleats depressed me. The shoes I liked could not really be worn with skirts, so my feet felt as covered and shaped as my legs. Shoes and clothes take you places, and my shoes and clothes made it difficult, nearly impossible, to go the neighborhood bar with my roommate or to the small, hip cafe or to any place that did not recognize and understand me. Like a dowdy twin always turning up to show others how paltry you could have been, my clothing swamped me.

For seven years I had gone to school in skirts, until one day I went to my junior English seminar in pants. I did not even make a real decision. After all my tortured study of the laws of modesty; the endless conversations with friends about whether a pious man would see beyond or (even better) understand such clothes; after all that worry over whether we would be loved and whether we were good, one day I got up and put on an old pair of pants.

I had thought that what I wanted was to wear sensible, unremarkable, modest pants. When I had talked about it with friends, male and female, that was what I had said. That was how I had known that these intentions too, rebellious as they seemed, were for the sake of heaven. They stemmed from innocent wants and needs, an interest in variety, my enthusiasm to run or climb. In high school for gym, we had worn skirts over sweatpants as we played baseball with a plastic bat in the parking lot around stationary cars. The boys had worn shorts and played basketball in the gym. My desire now did not even come near shorts; they seemed to me the same as nakedness. I thought only of pants. Not even jeans, which I knew bespoke too rugged a self, too natural, not conscious enough of myself as separate from others. Conceivably, as my friends and I argued, one could wear modest pants and still cover one's hair, still be respectable; but who wore jeans and covered her hair?

Yet when I found myself in the store later that week, in front of the mirror, 1991, it was in a pair of black Guess jeans. As if uncovering my own secret—that I had known all along there was no such thing as unremarkable pants, that "pants" meant remarkable—I had skipped all the intermediate stages—culottes, baggy pants, overalls, sweatpants, slacks—and gone to precisely the sort of pants that the books on modesty were really talking about. The pants they did not describe, in fear, but the pants they conjured.

But I did not allow the jeans to signify as everyone had believed they would. I abandoned nothing. In my jeans now, I prayed, I learned, I said blessings, I ate kosher food, I honored the sabbath, I continued to debate the rights of women in the heart of our Jewish community. And I went to class.

"Who shall measure the heat and violence of the poet's heart when caught and tangled in a woman's body!" Woolf had written seventy years earlier. When I had finished reading the slim volume *A Room of One's Own,* a single phrase rung in my ears: "torn asunder." In her short essay Woolf had repeated this phrase of violent division at least four times; my memory inscribed it on every page. In *A Room of One's Own, The Awakening, The House of Mirth*, back to *Middlemarch, Jane Eyre, Vindication*, in the voices of the feminist scholars who had written about them and in the voices of my professors at Barnard, I found a sympathetic community, women who knew what it was to be judged by sex, shut out of libraries. But they had crossed over, and I had not yet.

"Write the female body," my writing professor said. And though I was wearing my jeans, all I could think was, if I ever publish anything, will my hair in the jacket photo be real or a wig?

....

At nineteen, I was comforted for the struggles of my religious life by the discovery of George Eliot. After all the reading of my childhood and adolescence, I found in Eliot the author who wrote of ideas and experiences that might have been my own. It was not a general or illusory resemblance, the sort of parallel that might sustain itself only as long as the reading of the novel and the identification of the "I" of the narrator with the "I" that was myself. I imagined it to be vividly evident, something that even impartial outsiders, familiar with me and the novels, might acknowledge and remark upon as one notes an objective resemblance between siblings.

In Eliot's ardent young heroines, Maggie and Dorothea, I saw living women who struggled as I did with the want to be good and do good, the too early limitations because we were female, the impossible sacrifices that could never be made once and finished but seemed to require reenactment each waking day. Maggie Tulliver's "shadowy armies, slain and forever rising," were my landscape; she had all my sympathy, if she were still she and not me. Eliot's portraits of the sorrow and suffering that ushered in knowledge convinced me of what my spiritual and communal life seemed to be showing me: in a world built on convention and tradition, ardor meant pain and disappointment at least as often as it meant joy. Cultivating a wide sympathy for the other, living for others, meant struggling to satisfy the self, subduing the self.

But the beauty that came of it in Eliot's prose! My consolation for real suffering was the glory of her portraits and histories, the compact brilliance of her phrases—"for we all of us, grave or light, get our thoughts tangled in metaphors, and act fatally on the strength of them"—the magnitude of her philosophy, and the company she provided me.

I had not a moment of mistrust in George Eliot; between us there were no differences of opinion to overcome. Even as Eliot made me a better and better reader of her prose, a girl who saw herself more and more as Maggie, then Dorothea, I believed that I was the destined reader of her prose, the ear among many who could really hear and understand. In my love for Maggie and Dorothea I could imagine only that she loved them as I did; and in circular fashion, my love for them was inspired by the love I believed she felt for them.

My certainty that I understood what Eliot had intended was not wholly a product of fancy. She was the most circumspect writer I had ever encountered. In her long novels she left nothing undetailed or unspecified. Along the way she told one the value of those differences. I saw no ambiguity, hesitation, or self-contradictions corrupting the prose. In her clarity she was utterly knowable, and by some coincidence of fate I was the one who might know her best.

. . . .

My graduate studies began in Philadelphia in 1994 with a seminar devoted to George Eliot. My teacher was a woman whose name whispered itself before and after the great names on the banner that still flew in my mind, elegant red print, dignified white background. She was not a novelist nor a poet but a scholar of Victorian literature who had helped to invent an American feminist literary criticism. Without her and her counterparts there might have been no banner.

Before I could tell anything else, I could tell that she knew Eliot deeply. She told us that she would reread all the texts for class except *The Mill on the Floss* because she thought she might know it by heart; I did not doubt it. Just as my teachers of religious text could quote the objects of their study effortlessly, words and sentences flowed from her lips too, without pause or mistake. Even her paraphrases sounded like Eliot; she had got the voice and the rhythms.

She would have been a fine candidate for a true disciple except that in her rapid quotation, the famous phrases underwent a change. As if I had before me a hardened, criminal George Eliot, a child's nightmare of a mother who no longer defends you against the night but laughing, sends you out into it, the professor impersonated Eliot *cynically*. She coated Eliot's sayings in the mockery that can attend words that have crusted into cliché and truism: "But why always Dorothea?" Eliot's interruption of fluid storytelling, her radical appeal to move out of egocentrism into sympathy, to shift our attention from the blooming young heroine of *Middlemarch* to a withering, rayless husband, equally needful of readerly kindness, became in the professor's mouth not heroic or enlightened but sanctimonious and pedantic; finally, of dubious integrity. Hadn't the novel devoted the first hundred pages to Dorothea's perspective, fortifying and encouraging a commitment to her? Wouldn't the novel end well beyond the unloved man's death, fully focused again on Dorothea? Perhaps this was the way the novel rejected or despaired of empathy, even as it professed it as an ideal.

No one else in the classroom seemed shocked by what the professor said, by her suggestion that the action or structure or descriptive phrases of a novel could challenge what its omniscient narrator professed to believe, that novels had hidden underlives that their authors did not control but that we might detect and raise to the light.

In this casual, provocative talk we left behind a whole way of speaking. The question of whether Eliot's pronouncements were *right*, whether the things she said as narrator were *true* and would lead to a better world if followed, did not come up. No one, including me, spoke in the voice of gratefulness for the wisdom of George Eliot. And no one spoke in the voice of awe at her ability to dramatize her perceptions, to gradually impress upon the reader truths both recognizable and new, welcome and frightful: how deep and intertwined a history every action has; how little we know of the future, of ourselves, and each other when we set out with hope, and how much some of us come to know; how we cannot avoid living in the world, meeting our neighbors at moments when they look profoundly different, faces within faces, the dark, distinct aura of humility, the liquid circle of private meeting.

In the attempt to see Eliot in her historical and cultural context, to find within her novel's discontinuities telltale signs of the conflict and turmoil of mid-Victorian England and the development of the genre, we left aside the sort of reading I believed she had most hoped for. In a letter, Eliot had described her books as coming from her "heart of hearts"; she had hoped they would enter her reader's hearts. She had wished, with all the ambition of a Dorothea, to *do something* through her novels. To alter. In this new sort of study, critical and resistant, where was the place for ardor? For practice? For love?

....

Though my professor had said that she would reread the Eliot novels assigned for each class, when I made my attempt, I found I was barely capable of it. They were redolent of sleep or the half hour before sleep. When I took them down from the shelf, it was for the sort of book experience that is less about following attentively than about holding the volume in your hands, letting the half-remembered phrases wash over you. When you reach the end of the page, you are not entirely sure you have read to it, but you turn nonetheless; it is no matter; you have been there before.

In the light of such reading, writing a term paper at the end of the semester posed problems it had never posed before. I knew an ardent expression of sisterhood would not suffice for a term paper. One had to argue something, "shed light," teach, rather than show that one had been successfully taught. And I could not think of anything to say that did not seem wholly obvious, already specified and anatomized to the last detail by the resident scholar and narrator that was George Eliot. So I went to the library to see what others had said about George Eliot. The most recent critical work seemed to search the novel for contradictions rather than coherence, for variation rather than similarity, and for the signs of the construction of a novelistic world rather than its accurate reflection of reality. Because the best of the approaches I encountered were founded on strong textual evidence, evidence that I had learned in other contexts to consider fairly and respect absolutely, I had no choice but to admit their claims, even if I did not share their intuitions or motivating skepticism. When I went back to the novels now, I could see the origins of those claims as well as further evidence to bolster them.

Yet despite my intellectual commitments, only a powerful fantasy could solace me for the loss of my old devoted reading habit and allow me to make my way into this new, likely treacherous one. This fantasy, characteristic of the child-reader, spasmodically reincarnate in the adult-reader, this half-conscious desire that comes to some of us as we approach the end of a novel or oeuvre we have loved: the dream of not-having-read-yet. Of having this novel, this author, in our future rather than our past.

Surprised by the difficulty of writing on my favorite author, I made a plan. I would do my best to write a paper on the painful theft of precious manuscripts in Eliot's historical novel *Romola* and the fortuitous theft of golden coins in *Silas Marner*, the short, fablelike novel she had written in between her research for *Romola* and its composition. In comparing two works, perhaps I could give voice to something that had mattered deeply to Eliot but that she had found impossible or undesirable to say explicitly, something that she had said instead *between* her two works. Respectfully, loyally, I would try to connect the dots. Then, paper submitted, I would put aside her novels in order to renew them. I would honor George Eliot by applying myself to the literature of her times.

And so I spent the rest of my first year of graduate studies and the full year that followed reading the works of as many other Victorian authors as I could. But I was not quite prepared for what I discovered. In my early enthusiasm for *The Mill on the Floss*—the first Victorian novel I had ever read—every feature had seemed the mark of the author's private imagination, each one and all in their aggregate making their claims upon my admiration. But with each of the thirty novels I read over approximately a year, I realized that certain elements of *The Mill on the Floss, Adam Bede, Middlemarch* that had surprised and delighted me were, in fact, conventions.

Now, in the light of *Our Mutual Friend, Barchester Towers, Vanity Fair, North and South,* I saw how much there was that Eliot had not invented. I could see the stock characters: the fallen women, the noble women; the rakish, unemployed men; the misers and gamblers. I noted the standard occurrences of bankruptcy; legal trials; revelations of identity, kinship, and hidden pasts. Diamonds, china, horses, walking sticks. So this was the nineteenth century. Momentarily Eliot's finely drawn characters seemed like the generally molded figures of a mass-produced set of dolls.

Suddenly not only her novels but George Eliot's very name seemed a betrayal. A pseudonym we had retained as if to remind ourselves, to warn ourselves, that she craved mystery. Mary Ann Evans had taken a man's name for a woman's and simultaneously adopted an imaginary family. I could guess at the meaning of "George." Most likely it was a reference to her partner, George Henry Lewes, whose last name never became legally hers, though she considered him her husband and called herself "Mrs. Lewes." Perhaps the name nodded to George Sand as well.

But who was "Eliot"? The name that conjured for me the spirit of an iconoclastic woman had conjured only an unusually talented man of letters, perhaps even a cleric, to the English reading public. For a time—the time it took for George Eliot to become a novelist—the secret was well kept.

It seemed to me that George Eliot had slipped around like a girl climbing to the top of Butler Library under cover of night, ready to hang a day banner.

....

While reading Thackeray, Gaskell, Collins, Oliphant, Dickens, and Yonge, I offer to help the undergraduate Orthodox women at Hillel begin a women's prayer service in which they might learn the skills of leading and reading from the Torah scroll. We had a women's group at Brovender's; then I ran one at Columbia. The first such group was founded in New York more than twenty years ago, but it is only in the mid-1990s that this custom has begun to spread across the United States.

A growing number of Orthodox women are participating in such groups, though they face all sorts of objections. Some groups meet in private homes when rabbis forbid them space in the synagogue. Then they have to find private owners of a Torah scroll willing to lend it for the purpose of women's prayer. Often the women running the prayer groups have to do all their own telephoning and advertising since their rabbis will not announce the services from the pulpit, though the women have been members for decades. Other more liberal synagogues will grant the women a small chapel or the space of the library once a month. There are a few synagogues that champion these groups, but then they are discounted by others as not particularly Orthodox.

Many women prepare with enormous care for the meetings, often spending months learning a small section of the Torah reading that their husbands, fathers, brothers, and sons could learn in an hour. Though most of them have been attending synagogue all their lives, they have no experience here. All of a sudden, what has always seemed as familiar as blood is as mysterious and undercover. Now that there is no *mehitza* from behind which to follow the prayer led by men, the difference the *mehitza* has created and the knowledge it has prevented become meaningful even to those women who have always said that they do not mind, that they find prayer just as significant without taking an active role in it.

The simplest of procedures confound women who have prayed all their lives yet are now leading prayer for the first time. Doing and watching, we discover, are not the same thing. How does one roll the Torah to the right place? We cannot remember whether you say the prayer for the sick before or after the Torah reading is completed. Does the woman who has been called to the Torah stand on the right side of the reader or the left side? When does she go back to her seat?

While these questions of procedure can be answered simply, part of our disorientation is the confusion as to what is allowed us as women. *Halakhic* Judaism is not a system that condones extras: often if one is not obligated in a ritual, one is prohibited, the rationale being that one is preventing the obligated person from fulfilling his obligation or pointing to a deficiency among the obligated community. For a woman to read among men might suggest that there is no man capable of reading.

Now, in 1995 at Penn Hillel, two women and I gather to plan for our group. Though the three of us have participated in such groups before, we raise questions we need to resolve before our first meeting. For instance: if our *hazanit*, our leader, recites aloud the repetition of the silent prayer, what should she do about the section called *kedushah*, which requires the male quorum in order to be recited? When we pose this question and others to an Orthodox rabbi assigned to advise us, he does not experience our urgency. No specialist on these issues, he tells us that in all matters that do not have to do with the prayers of holiness, which we, as women without ten men, are forbidden to say, we can do whatever we want. It is not just that the stakes are not high; there simply *are* no stakes. Since our service has no legal standing—it might as well never have happened, the rabbi says, trying to explain—we can make all the mistakes we want.

And so we return to our own study of the legal texts. Yet our questions move away from legal matters. What do we do about the fact that the entire liturgy in all prayer books in use in Orthodox synagogues is written in the male gender? It is not the language for God that we are talking about, simply the descriptive, gendered language the leader uses in calling people to the Torah, then asking God to bless them afterwards. And another query: though we substitute the blessing "Blessed are you God, who has made me according to His will" for the blessing men recite thanking God for not having made them women, often a shadow passes over the group at that early moment in the service. Maybe we should recite those prayers silently?

When the student leadership of the Orthodox *minyan* (prayer community) is told that we are planning a weekly women's prayer service, all our own questions come to a grinding halt. Nice, polite young men and a woman, nineteen years old, tell us that we can have no group until they investigate its Jewish legal status. Next semester, one of them is slated to be my student.

Here are the alternatives as we see them: if we simply ignore this new obstacle and found the group under the auspices of Hillel, a nondenominational Jewish student organization, rather than associate ourselves with the Orthodox *minyan* at Hillel, we can hold our first meeting tomorrow. But if we do that, a good number of the Orthodox undergraduate women, for whom we have founded the group, will no longer feel comfortable—or brave—enough to attend. As it is, they run the risk of being branded radical feminists and losing the sympathy of many of their peers. On the other hand, if we are simply a women's group run by Hillel, then the non-Orthodox women who come will want to know why we are not holding a service equivalent to the one that ten men would hold: why, if we are ten women, are we not saying the holy prayers that ten men may say together?

In the end we decide to stay Orthodox. *Halakha* binds the three of us, and it binds the women who may want to join us for prayer. Conservative women or Reform women have no shortage of places to pray. Orthodox women always need one more venue, always need a new option. If this student situation is more demeaning than most, it is nonetheless familiar. To be on the edge of something often means still needing the *hekhsher*, the kosher certification, of those closer to the center, of the majority.

I know all this, and I want the younger women to come to our services. Still, the phrase of my college days comes back to me: "For the sake of heaven": *l'shem shamayim.*

The cacophony and dispute and even the disgrace: are those considered heavenly tributes?

....

We met on the first morning of graduate school, both helplessly seeking an elusive classroom and the course: Renaissance Epic. Within three months of shared study, the hours of talk born of shared experience and reading, we had come to know each other well enough to exchange writing. John gave me five poems and I gave him "Binah."

Almost a full year later, many months of talk later, he offers me the sort of gift I have never received. Time has made this gift, time and a labor of thought. John has written twenty-five pages, bound them and laminated the cover. This small book is his response to my work. He has composed a critical dialogue between characters he has invented and named.

As soon as I begin to read him, I understand that "Binah" is no longer mine. I have written a text that, it now appears, I barely know. As well as writing about the struggles of Jewish women, I have written by omission, elision, and metaphor, John's characters contend, about the intifada, about the territories of land Israel occupies against the desires of Palestinians. In describing the men guarding the Torah "as if" they are "at war," preparing the page of Gemara with the circumspection they would use were an enemy to approach a piece of land, I have written politics into spirit, history into fable. The columns of the Torah I call furrows of earth, the acquisition of Torah I speak of as the conquest of such contested land.

I thought I was writing of a conflict between Jewish men and women. Simultaneously I wrote of the conflict between Jews and Arabs. A Jewish woman with no Beit Midrash to welcome her, my story criss-crosses the story of Arabs deprived of rightful homes, epic birthplaces. I am the Jew, but I am also the woman. My identity is not single; I could cultivate ties to more than one cause.

When we talk of John's poems, which I find difficult to understand—there is rarely a central consciousness or character—he shows me that each word comes from a root; that root has myriad branches. Each phrase he uses takes his poem in seventy directions. He writes, I learn, in a science of language, with a dictionary on hand letting him into the mysteries of all the things one word can mean. His interest resides in the puzzles made by the meetings of those meanings. Each word links back to earlier forms that engendered it; links to others nearby, within his own work, that sound alike or mean alike; links to others outside his work, in the writings of different writers, who widen the circle of his meanings still further.

He tries, when he writes, to consider etymologies, metaphors, allusions, puns. He is always reading himself as he writes. Self-divided, he investigates the system that is his own prose. But he wants me to read his poems so he can learn more about them. He is made happy by knowing that language exceeds him, that I will see what he could not, that what he intended may be the least of what I find or, more likely, may elude me altogether.

I try to teach him his poems.

....

In the middle of my second year of graduate school, I take myself to the women's service when it meets. Again the quiet walks through sleep-laden campus, the sense that only a strange species of university student rises so early to pray.

But a change comes to separate me from the familiarity of daily, weekly, yearly rhythms. For the first time in twelve years, I do not have a *havruta,* a regular study partner with whom to work at a text slowly, regularly, and diligently. At home in my own apartment, I look at all the holy books on my bookcase and do not open them either. I tell myself that if I would only choose one and start to read, I would become absorbed.

But I walk to the other bookshelf instead, read another novel, more literary theory, anthropology, philosophy. I have lost the discipline I once possessed in abundance, the ability to do what is at first difficult toward an end whose rightness will express itself in the purest pleasure.

One day I receive a call from the university Hillel: the student who gives the weekly lesson on the Torah portion is ill; can I fill in for him? Though I have not opened a holy book in months, I accept out of habit. You do not turn down an honor associated with the Torah, a simple fact.

At home in the early dark afternoon, my home lit only by a lamp, I sit with my old volume of Exodus. In this small circle of light, darkness surrounding, the trouble of living recedes; it yields to the pressing problems of the text.

I teach for an hour and a half on the chapters that describe the breaking of the tablets and Moses' plea before God not to destroy the people and set him up as a nation in their stead. When speaking to God, Moses loved Israel; when speaking to Israel, Moses loved God. Above, God was engraving God's gift; below, Aaron engraved his own. Then the silent, fat, and golden calf turned to dirty drinking water as Moses took the stonework of God, such as had never before been seen—writing with light, writing that leapt from stone to freedom—and shattered it at the bottom of the mountain. All things made were destroyed, broken down to their constituent materials—fragmentary, testimonial, then lost or perhaps only hidden.

While I am teaching, my mind is alive, and questions come to me with an urgency that encourages further study. But when the class is over, I walk home alone and replace the book on its shelf between its companion volumes. One must close a book to shelve it, and I do; I silence its voices.

The Sages say, "He who does not add to his study, takes away." I know this; still, I do not learn.

. . . .

I cannot find the gold necklace I am used to wearing every day. When I turned eight, my parents gave me a small, rectangular box; inside, a plush green velvet surface upon which a gold necklace rested. It was my name in the traditional Hebrew block letters, whose right angles and uncompromising diagonals had been transformed into beautiful, curving shapes that dangled and came together unexpectedly.

Aleph, yod, lamed, nun, hey: אילנה. *The word for a tree, Ilan, with the suffix of hey, the letter that takes a noun, in this case me, the person, the body, and makes it female: a girl.*

The letters were beautiful. The yod *and* hey *were smaller than the other three letters, but met each other at the same height, forming the word* Yah. *The name of God one is forbidden to pronounce, even to write, so that in colloquial speech and writing, the* yod *becomes a* quf, *interrupting the divine name, redirecting it as "qah." In the case of my name, the* lamed *and* nun *interceded between the two letters, restraining the attraction of the magnetic characters, whose union is believed sufficient to spark the divine fire.*

The aleph *and* lamed, *though taller, met each other at the same level too, forming the syllable and word* el, *which could mean both the minor preposition "to" and the imperative* al, *do not. As in the*

Psalmist's plea, "Do not forsake us," אל תשליכנו: Al tashlikheinu. *Or Abraham's request that the godly messenger visiting him not leave without resting under his shelter,* אל נא תעבר מעל עבדך: Al na ta'avor mei'al avdekhah. *Finally, the* aleph-lamed *of my name spelled another name for God, as in Beit* El, בית אל, *the house of God where Jacob slept with a rock for a pillow and saw in his sleep angels ascending and descending a ladder that spanned earth and sky.*

In a language rich with appellations, nicknames, euphemisms, and attributes for God, it is not surprising that my name contains two. It contains as well the word eyn or ayin. Aleph, yod, nun: אין: "there is none." As in the hymn that closes Shabbat and festival prayer, "Eyn K'eloheinu," there is none like our God: אין כאלהינו. Or ayin, nothingness, as in the phrase of the medieval philosophers who strove to prove against the ancient Greek thinkers that God's initial creation of the world had been, miraculously, "yesh mei 'ayin," *ex nihilo*, יש מאין, and not "yesh m'yesh," something from something, יש מיש.

Or ayin: the homonym for the Hebrew word that means "eye," the organ of sight, which in turn is the English homonym for "I," the slight, slim, economical character that represents the self.

Eyn: there is none. Ayin: nothingness. Ayin: the eye. The eye: the I.

Ayin *means absence.* "Havah li banim, vi'im ayin, metah anokhi": הבה לי בנים ואם אין מתה אנכי. *Rachel's memorable words to her husband Jacob. The standard translation reads "Give me children, else I die." Yet that translation effaces the paradoxical presence of absence at the center of desperate Rachel's cry. "Vi'im ayin, metah anokhi." If* ayin *holds sway, then I am dead. If in the place where meaning should live, nothingness reigns instead, then I am as good as dead.*

"Anokhi adonai elohechah": אנכי ה' אלהיך. *It is I, anochi, who am the Lord, your God. This is the first of the ten commandments.*

"Vi'im ayin, metah anokhi": ואם אין מתה אנכי. *If there is nothing-ness, it is the death of myself and the death of the Almighty. It is the death of I.*

I cannot find my necklace and it means all this.

. . . .

Perhaps I had stopped reading the Bible because I was no longer sure I knew what its words meant. The Bible was a document whose interpretation shaped many more lives than any novel in history ever had. And each person of faith implicitly or explicitly made the claim that what he or she derived from its reading was sacred, sanctioned. You did not have to be a fundamentalist arguing for literal readings—for instance, that God had given the land of Israel to the Jews—to claim that you had penetrated God's intent. Each of us read the Bible, ancient document, in faith.

I was no different than any other interpreter. All of us, *darshening,* interpreting, claiming that God saw it as we did, that we could penetrate to His intention on the basis of His word. But I had learned that intention was no simple matter— my professor said one thing about George Eliot, I said another, a third critic said a third. There was a hard kernel, the words of the text, and you could not make them say anything, but even with that hard kernel, you could make multiple cases for meaning. Then it was a matter of weighing those cases, choosing the one that seemed most comprehensive, most attentive to language, most logical given what else you knew. Even the standards for choosing proliferated greatly. There was no way to arbitrate finally to the satisfaction of anyone but yourself or the interest you represented. Interpretation always said more about the reader than the writer.

Yet this was not a reason to abandon Torah study. Though I had learned the depth of this problematic from literary theory, I had watched students of the Torah offer different interpretations of the same passages countless times. From youth I had

been told that each year we could study the Torah anew because its meanings were multiple, infinite. I knew that the
rabbis of the Talmud had affirmed without hesitation that the
final meaning of the Torah was not in God's hands and that
God Himself, *b'khvodo u'vatzmo*, בכבודו ובעצמו, in all His glory,
had ordained that human interpretation must triumph over
divine. According to this passage, God, in all His Honor and
His Glory, bows to the interpretation of His students, even
when it is at odds with His own perfect understanding, and
laughs, not cries, when He admits—no, when He exults—"My
children have won over Me."

I could cite too the ancient as well as contemporary com-
mentators who took great pains to read the story of revelation
on Mount Sinai as not one public teaching but multiple, private revelations, with God's voice reaching each human ear
and heart according to its own powers of understanding and
need. And perhaps most poignant of all, the sentence I learned
so early from the Midrash: God looked in the Torah, then
created the world: כך היה הקב״ה מביט בתורה ובורא את העולם.
According to this Midrash, even God Himself, the author of
the Torah, bowed to the independent authority of the text He
had written, let the book itself guide Him in creation. God
read, then created. The book, once written, says this Midrash
to me, is never entirely one with its author; only in thought can
the thinker and the thought be one.

Yet despite the room in my tradition for such complicated
notions of intention and authorship, it was not *my* interpretations of the Bible—or the interpretations of anyone of my sex,
no matter how learned—that those Midrashim were honoring
and protecting. It was the interpretive power of the rabbis—a
power that slid immediately into legislative power—to which
the Talmud referred when it said God laughed in pleasure.
And the wives of those rabbis had given birth to sons who had
given birth to sons who had not expanded the notion of "sage"
to include women. It was men who ruled over interpretation

and its translation into the material conditions against which I was struggling. If I could not believe that the decisions they were making necessarily reflected God's will but revealed their own human, contingent intellects and dispositions, I no longer felt bound to obey.

....

"Read with me? 'A Valediction'?"

I have loved Donne's poem since I was twelve years old. I encountered it first in a series of novels written for girls: earnest, romantic, bookish girls. By now I know that Donne is not to be trusted. Like other famous lyric I's, this one too cannot be taken at face value. Donne's worldly-wise speaker is a player who is talking his beloved into waiting around for him while he sets sail; he lets her know in advance that he won't cry when he leaves. If you cry, he tells her, it means your love is shallow.

I know how to read this poem like a student of literature, also like a feminist. But tonight all I want to do is read in earnest mode, to sidestep the connivances. I know, I know, but tonight I want to read this poem as a real love poem.

"But we by a love so much refined/That our selves know not what it is/Inter-assurèd of the mind,/Care less, eyes, lips, and hands to miss."

We read aloud, slow and deliberate, switching off stanzas. And as we read and I listen to myself, then to John, I think back to twelve. Twelve, that magical girl-age, made of the numbers one and two, side by side, as if contiguity is easy; as if union is easy.

But today I am more than twice twelve; I am twenty-five. The idea of a love that cares less eyes, lips, and hands to miss begs pause, not only from a cynical reader, but from a loving one too.

If one truly cared less, one wouldn't name the parts. One wouldn't slow the poem to put unusual stresses over each part of the body that the speaker mentions only to dismiss. Eyes. Lips. Hands. Like commanding a listener to forget a story, but in the process of commanding, telling the whole story again, replete with delights.

At twenty-five, I am not earnest; nor am I cynical. I seem to be reading this poem at the precise moment when its problems, its paradoxes, are still powerfully mysterious yet recognizable to me. Tonight the poem itself seems to be about equipoise, about the realistic space between earnest and cynical.

Here's the problem, the one that the earnest girl can't see, in love with the idea of the meeting of the minds, and that the cynic, unwilling to believe in love or goodness, can't respect. Here's the serious crux of my poem. Love might need the body; even the truest love might falter without it.

In the face of that knowledge, a worldly poem records an honest desire, stirring and impossible as all desires, that it be otherwise. That it not matter. That we not miss eyes, hands, and lips so badly that separation attenuates our love or that our love brings us more pain than satisfaction.

"Our two souls therefore which are one."

I knew it was beautiful half my lifetime ago: the rapture of imagined union.

And now what is beautiful to me is the immediate turning back in the very next stanza to wonder what happens "if," after all, "they be two."

. . . .

When I was a child, my school met for a year in a Church of Christ. Strange: twenty Jewish children gathering daily to study in a home not their own. But that year, 1977, there was no available space in Jewish Ann Arbor that met school code. The church offered, and parents and teachers said a grateful yes. The school was two years old; if it wanted to open its doors for a third school year, they would be church doors.

I recall no cross or steeple, no organ or hanging vestments; what I remember is the white sheets. Mondays they would go up, Fridays they would come down. We shared our classroom with invisible children who came on Sundays to Sunday school, to church. We never saw them, and they never saw us, but we knew they came and sat at our desks, looked up at our blackboard. Perhaps they wondered at our foreign script, the strange Hebrew letters, black and impossible next to the simplicities of ABC; above our cubbies, our strange names, both first and last; a calendar of English months overwritten by foreign holy days and dates.

On Mondays, when we returned, things would always be out of place. Pens or scissors would be missing. Books and games would have switched places; a bookmark would point to the wrong page. Occasionally, signs of a pogrom would greet us: open boxes on the floor, scattered puzzle pieces. Hebrew and English books lying open or face down, with spines cracking, cracking. These signs were how we knew the invisible children had been and gone. We worked in code. There was never a note; no friendliness passed between us.

Who was the child who sat at my desk? Did she or he have glasses as I did? Did she raise the top of my desk and see all that was mine? Why did we pass this way, like ghosts of each other?

Because they came only on Sundays, they kept no possessions in our classroom. All they had was what was under the white sheets. Jesus Christ and large crosses, much larger than any I had ever seen. Blood, long hair, sheep and landscapes of old walls and towers, grassy paths and hills. It is Israel, isn't it?

Jesus was not visible when we were learning. The white sheets announced his suffering absence, and we grew accustomed to their whiteness. We knew we were foreigners in the church, that we had to be on our best behavior to keep up the "good relationship." But it was a relationship to blankness, to invisible, marauding children who made our teachers miserable on Monday mornings. "The Church," our parents called it; meaning what? Meaning the blood and long hair? Meaning the quiet pastor whom we saw at times in the hall? Meaning the congregation that I was told met on Sundays to do I-did-not-know-what?

I learned nothing about the institution that had graciously provided a home for our small, wandering school. Perhaps the adults spoke to each other; they must at least have negotiated terms. The teachers must have complained to the Church about the worst of the Mondays. But the children never met.

White sheets stood between us and them, protecting us from their blood and their stories.

. . . .

My mother fears for me. Other than John, she is the only person in the world who touches my face. In this way my mother and I have the intimacy of lovers.

My mother's fear corrupts my love for John. Though I have often mentioned his name to her, she never asks for him as she does for my other friends: two Rachels, a Rebecca, an Amir. John's name resembles my brother's, Jonathan, and I remember my mother's worry when we were children that her son would turn into John with an H; I remember her antipathy for that Christian name.

My mother cannot bring herself to acknowledge my life with John, even when she calls me late at night and early in the morning and I am not home. I reason that if she truly did not know where I was, she would call the police. Somewhere, then, she knows it all.

One day on the phone she says to me that she stops in the middle of things she is doing, in the middle of the day, the middle of the week, and thinks about me with a kind of terror, as if I were in physical danger, as if my life were threatened. She lies in bed at night thinking of the child I was. Thinking of how I may abandon everything she labored and joyed to give me. She remembers all the Hebrew records, the songs I grew up singing as if I were a child in Jerusalem or Tel Aviv, not Midwestern America; the holiday smells and recipes; the way I learned to crack an egg into a glass to check for blood spots before pouring it into the batter; the exhausting, wonderful work of grinding cup after cup of nuts for the Passover *haroset* before the days of the Cuisinart; the hours we spent in synagogue, when I first made sense of the foreign letters, found the ones in my name scattered among the words of prayers I now say by heart.

There is no child for her without those memories; she cannot extract from them some Secular Child she can love as well as she loves me, a girl who learned to read only English and not Hebrew too, who danced ballet and played the piano like countless other American little girls but did not pray at her side. What does it mean, my mother is asking, that everything I saw, heard, smelled, touched, tasted—her lighting candles each Friday night; my father preparing the weekly Torah reading, comparing two renditions of *Kol Nidre* as Yom Kippur approached; the spices reviving me as Shabbat was ushered from our home; the fringes of my father's *tallit* against my face as I leaned against him standing in the synagogue; the wine on my tongue, the bitter herbs, the honey, apples, almonds, Torah—now amounts to nothing?

For my mother there is no child to match the woman she thinks I am becoming. She is sure she knew a child, did not make her up; she is equally sure that a *dybbuk* has entered me, an evil outsider, a silent, magical violence that if she could, she would hunt and then kill, like our great-great grandmothers would have done, all in a band, with broomsticks and chants, in their small, now lost, towns and villages.

If she asked, I would tell her about the aloneness of forgetting to pray some mornings because I am not in my place. In John's home there are no prayer books on the shelves to remind me it is morning and that it is my task to arise with energy to carry out the will of my Father in Heaven, as the Mishnah has it. I would tell her about the way John can identify Rashi on a page of Gemara; about the way my kitchen remains as kosher as ever and that John and I drink only kosher wine; that I have paper plates and utensils at his house that do the work of reminding me that we are supposed to see each other as alien and untouchable. I would let her know that Shabbat is lonely and intimate at the same time, intimate in company and conversation, lonely in holiness and solitary prayer. I would tell her how not having a family of my own makes Jewish life impossible, how faith seems stupid without children, husbands, mothers-in-law. How there is no joy, comfort, or pleasure in banding together with other single Jews my own age, pretending we are a family, assigning the postures we learned in our earliest childhood games of playing Shabbat, games that began with rolling out pretend-dough for challah and ended with pointing to one boy and one girl, designating them the parents: *You can be the Ima, you can be the Abba.*

But she doesn't ask, and I don't offer. We enter a silent hostile zone, silent on her part, hostile on mine. I blame everything on her. I blame her for all my friends' being simply, untroubledly married while I remain without an appropriate partner; she is the one who raised me to need things outside of what it seems I can have. I blame her for encouraging me to write and then running from the job of looking at what I have put on paper, and I blame her for teaching me to read, celebrating the look of characters on the page and their sound in our mouths as we read aloud together, everywhere, on the beach, in the backyard, in bed, in the kitchen, on the sofa, during storms, on snowy days, in the middle of the night, on airplanes. I blame her for taking me to the library to gather new books as many times a week as I needed, and I blame her for buying me ice cream when I got my first library card. For enrolling me in summer reading games and helping me add each book's title to the list of books read, list of my pride; for subscribing to children's literary magazines with me and sending off my early contributions to them, then making dittos of the poem I published to send to my grandparents for their refrigerator. I blame her for having had lots of books in our house; for reading herself and allowing me to see her reading;

for having herself been an English major studying Henry James; for reading to me from *Oliver Twist,* a Victorian novel, before bedtime when I was eight; for buying me books and books and more books for birthdays and holidays and inscribing each one from herself and my father, dating each one so that they stand today as my biography on the bookshelf. I blame her for valuing books; for treating them well; not writing in them, not throwing them out or ripping pages out of them; not giving them away even when she has not opened them in many years; for saving them instead and putting them in prominent places in our home while some of my friends' parents put televisions and video games there.

But I am the daughter of a father too, and it is because of what he gave me—a knowledge become unusable—that I have stopped going to synagogue. When I was ten, he taught me the skill of chanting the sacred texts. Because he taught me well, I soon became able to translate the words of the Torah as they appeared in the books I studied at school into memorable fragments of music. I have this advantage, one for which other women, raised more traditionally, express their admiration, because my father raised me as a Jewish boy would have been raised. He raised me, a girl, to belong, to know, to sing, to pass down.

Summer comes and with it the decision to travel. I will leave Philadelphia, John, this miserable joy, and return to Israel.

I came from a predominantly intellectual rather than mystical tradition of Judaism, and in the halls of my high school yeshiva, I had been taught that the best antidote to doubt and anger was study: answers lay in the wisdom of older generations. We studied to gain knowledge more than to give testimony to our faith in the ultimate worth of the object of our study and even less to sink into the comforts of the vanilla page, its fantasies and dreams. Unlike the rabbis who came before us, we did not indulge in flights of fancy, in imagined dialogues with the Master of the Universe, in time travel and the suspension of the properties of the natural world. We followed lines of thought; we reasoned and considered. We used dictionaries to find the etymologies of words, then recorded our findings like scientists.

As moderns, furthest from the light of revelation, we were not free to speculate and create, to be irresponsible, untraditional, even wild, as a pathway to achievements that could not be made through the brain. We would hear the story of the rebbe who rose at dawn in the mornings before Rosh Hashanah and instead of praying the *Selihot* prayers, chopped wood in disguise for a needy old woman, or the story of the small, ignorant shepherd boy whose reed flute prayer alone allowed the great rabbi of his town to close the Yom Kippur worship with confidence in the community's redemption, and we would nod our heads. But all around us we saw books, not flutes; we prayed regularly and did not give ourselves over to the impulses borne in upon us by the world around. Visiting the sick and elderly was important, but we did that once a week, while we studied Torah five hours a day. We had no study of music or dance and one semester of art. We studied no mystical traditions, and to this day I have read no writings of any of the great Hasidic masters, while I have studied volumes of Jewish transformations of Aristotelian philosophy and the intricacies of Talmudic argumentation.

Yet each year on Chanukah or Simhat Torah, occasionally on Rosh Hodesh, we would dance together at school celebrations of the holidays. And in the dance and song, dictionaries would fall to the side. Our teachers, who were so demanding, so exacting of us in our knowledge, would show us the pulsing heart that made the whole project vital. The men would sweat and their foreheads would shine; the women would push the pins back to secure their trembling wigs as the circles, men and women separate, whirled around and the song rose in the room.

This, I guessed, was why it mattered at all that we studied. This was the elusive love of God or love of Israel that we read about, the explanation for the hours and hours devoted to intellectual rigor applied not to the novels of the nineteenth century or to cell biology, but to the Torah. The song and dance, the giving of the body's strength, the freedom of holding hands with other girls who were not your friends, whose names you might not know, whom you might fear or dislike, women who graded you and disciplined you but now pressed your hand with their fingers as if all were different in this family celebration with the Torah at the center. All this happened like a dream a few times a year.

Just as rarely a teacher would come into the classroom and say, "Write as if you were Sarah; imagine Jacob's struggle until dawn with the mysterious man." Then again, but less so, the bounds of the intellect were loosed, and like the rabbis of the Midrash but in a modern voice, I would speak the unwritten, add to the holy. But even in that freedom, responsibility was all; I wrote defensively, basing myself in interpretations I had read or the hints my practiced eye had learned to see in the always taciturn text.

In this world, doubt was its own category instead of being seen as part of life. It was a problem to be solved, not a natural, expected phase in my life as a person of faith. Calmness was missing, the calmness and surety that doubt and change were not catastrophic and that they might be best healed or at least addressed wordlessly, through the spirit.

I came to Israel this time, then, in part as the product of my intellectual religious heritage. But I came in rebellion against that tradition too, with a mystical belief in the power of a blessed land and its air to bring greater love of God. I traveled with the desire for Hebrew and an equally strong desire for a silence from all the parties left behind—a silence that would allow me not only to know my heart but to purify it.

············

My summer study was the Book of Numbers, the second-to-last of the Five Books of Moses; its Hebrew title, במדבר, Ba'midbar, means literally "in the desert." Endless stories of the impossibilities of faith for the children of Israel. When God fed them bread, they asked for meat. When God promised that the land was good, that He would help them conquer it, nervously they sent their spies. Rudely they challenged the power of Moses, God's chosen one. They set out to battle when God had warned them that He would not go up in their midst.

Fiery punishments followed. Deadly plagues. Rebels fell through a crack in the earth, God's newest creation. The people learned that only Joshua and Caleb, God's lone faithful ones, would enter the Promised Land. God's final, lurid warning: in this desert will be strewn the corpses that were once the children of Israel.

I took pleasure in Ba'midbar, painful and unrelenting as it was, because it was the opposite of Passover. Cheerfully, almost raucously, from the pillowed seats of redemption, amid glasses overflowing with red wine and tablecloths stained from the excess, we had sung: Had God only taken us from Egypt but not judged our enemies, it would have been enough. Had God only torn the sea but not brought us through its path upon dry land, it would have been enough. Had God only brought us to Sinai, but not given us the Torah, we would have been satisfied. How grateful we are for the Sabbath and for the Temple, but we would have been grateful without them too. Everything we have been given, all gifts, utterly superfluous. In slightly drunken memory of where we never were, we give back gifts with abandon.

But in the desert, long before Israel, before Sinai, before the Temple, there was not enough of anything. There was a shortage of faith between God and Israel and a shortage of love. In the shadows of Egypt, God and Israel looked at each other and saw absence instead of presence. Absence turned to hatred, the certainty that one was hated, then the hatred for the other.

....

Maybe when I leave, I will never come back.

The prayer would go like this:

To turn my back on the country, the land, its people, and return home without regret. Not to mark my last breaths of air, my last footsteps on land before I step onto the airplane. Not to listen to the sounds of Israeli radio until the last possible moment, until the station does not come in anymore and the songs and language I want cannot be had. For once, to leave Israel without sadness. To be glad to leave the land where God's eyes travel always. To elude those eyes forever. To believe not just that they are unseeing, as the ear is unhearing, but to believe that there are no such eyes.

There never have been.

....

Shabbat was slow to come.

All around me, Jerusalem made the Sabbath. The siren rang; the sky turned pink; cars desisted from the roads; men walked in the streets to their neighborhood synagogues; activity slowed and finally ceased.

I consider the stories of my childhood. Hanaleh, the lost little girl whose beautiful white dress turns black from the coal of a beggar she has helped. She sits on a rock, alone, forsaken, but Shabbat comes for her, even in her darkened dress. *My mother tells me the story, then we sing the beautiful, slow song about the Shabbat Queen, entreating her to come, promising welcome.* I remembered too the character of Yosef-Mokir-Shabbat, Joseph-Who-Honors-the-Sabbath: the poor man who spends all he owns on a grand fish for Shabbat, then opens it to find a magnificent pearl as reward for his loving faith. White dresses, beggars, fish, angels, and the Sabbath Queen, whose visit was not automatic but brought about by a week's labor and intention, a life lived to merit her presence.

But I could not bring the Sabbath anymore. If I were part of any fairy tale, it was an inverse Chagall painting in which the extra Sabbath soul floating above me was not a soul after all, but a wraith, ghost-empty.

When Friday evenings came, I went to sleep. In the apartment I shared with two girls, I closed my door on food and wine, company, my friends and family in Israel. Pain came in being with others on Shabbat; I knew the Sabbath had come for them, yet I could not bring it for me.

Though I could not sit close to others, conversing with affection, singing with conviction, I could walk long distances. On the fifth Friday night I was in Israel, I put on an old, simple dress, took my prayer book and set off to the Kotel, the Western Wall. If I could not welcome the Sabbath, I could welcome the loneliness of that site, where every Jew seemed poor and stray and where, unlike in the synagogue, our unity consisted of allowing each other the one thing we might have to offer, the privacy of prayer.

At the Kotel I would stand at the back, far from the wall itself, pull one of the heavy, weather-beaten chairs next to the barrier separating men and women, and be part of the haphazard spectacle the nonbelievers came to see every Friday night: Jews welcoming the Sabbath out of doors, a matter of local color. I would hold my prayer book and slowly begin to say the appropriate prayer for evening.

I said this prayer at the Kotel and finished the rest of the evening prayer service. Then, as I always did, I sat quietly, just to be in that place without disturbance. I listened to the old women raise their voices in cries and demands and the young women whisper their prayers as if to lovers, and I watched the girls stand at their mothers' sides as their mothers showed them how to kiss the wall, how to push their bodies against it and whisper into its crevices, how to be women here.

I let these sights and sounds surround me; then I neared the wall and stopped a foot short of it. There was no free space against it; women crowded next to each other in order to find themselves small openings. I was not impatient but willing to wait to arrive. I thought of my mother and how she always hurried to the wall, never warmed up as I did at the back. I thought of her urgency to touch the wall, to be there already, to have been standing there. I waited still.

After a few minutes, a young woman backed away from the wall; her eyes were wet. Here every woman seemed a Leah. I took this sister's place and tentatively, even tensely, allowed my body to rest against the wall. With my fingers and the palm of my hand, I felt the stones, and the words rose from me reflexively, calming me: *hafakhta misp'di,* הפכת מספדי למחול לי: "You have turned my lament into dance, You have loosed my sackcloth and girded me with joy, Lord God; I will praise You forever."

By heart I recited this psalm and others as I had always prayed, in a mixture of concentration and abstraction. Above or below the understanding of the words that raced from my lips—"Who builds Jerusalem," "Who loves His people, Israel," "the Lord is One," "maker of peace and creator of all,"—I prayed a wholly personal prayer for the safety of the people I loved. First, I prayed for my brother. This meant an intense thought of him, a vision of him that was like a hollow outline, in which he could do many things, be many ages, all at once. I could see his face and not see his face.

But I could barely find him without the ancient Hebrew words of psalms and blessings spinning themselves from me. In their current I could risk thinking the object of thought without the distance, the safety, of a preposition. Instead of thinking *of, about,* or *for,* I could think the thing or person itself until it grew so large it was invisible. The everything that was nothing, it could swallow me. In this world of subjects and no predicates, no end, no exit, there was only, always, the end of the psalm, the close of the blessing.

In the current of the psalms, words of anonymity, I tried to think my family, friends, teachers, students, as I always had before. And God was a distant God. I was afraid that I could not bring the people I loved before his eye to awaken his notice. I raised the vision of those I loved to be greeted by nothing but my own sharp fear, the fear of danger and contingency, a huge world in which we were all too far apart, in which harm could strike before any one of us could intervene or even offer old, poor love. I found I could not pray for justice and mercy, the two attributes from which the world was created, so I searched for something narrower, something for which I could pray wholeheartedly.

I prayed against senseless death—car accidents, children running heedless across busy streets, candles or lamps left burning in the small apartments of elderly people. The sorrows I could concentrate on were limited to those that seemed to have no conscious, responsible agents. Blunders and stupidities, lapses of judgment and skill, they arose of inevitable weakness and damning bad luck, not evil will. I could not wish in any truly hopeful or visionary way for an end to war's intentional violence, or crime's necessary deprivation of another person's possessions or life. I stood far from the subject of human treachery and imagined guilt, blame, and moral responsibility in their most attenuated yet frightful form: a child's drawing of his family tree, one branch leading to another, each branch stemming from a previous one.

I could not judge anymore what I believed should happen, and I could not ask God for things whose possibility I had ceased to credit: peace between people who do not love but rather alarm, confuse, and thwart each other; simple choices as to where and how to live and spend one's time; the containment of hurt inflicted by one person on another; a world that works in understandable, rewarding, viable ways. I did not expect that anymore, so I did not bother to think of it or pray for it.

For nothing unnatural did I pray. I desired my elderly grandparents not to suffer pain, but I no longer desired that they not die, that they live forever. I put aside bargain thought, bargains that expand infinitely and are guaranteed never to satisfy: let my grandparents at least live to see me married; then, let them live to see me a mother; then, a mother of two children. There is no end to such thinking. I no longer imagined any promised lands in which we were home free: if only I could have *this*, if only I could live in this way, if only I could live with such a lover, if only I could bear a child, if only I could be successful in the career I chose, if only I could write the book I imagined today, if only I might be healthy, if only I might have enough money to have some to give away and not want, if only I could speak to this one in such a way that he would understand. . . . The language of a life of narrow margins and escapes, gifts and breathless thank-yous, and then new desires, surprising in their insistence; language of the noncontinuous life, the life in stops and starts. *If only*—beginning sentences that trail off, that don't end, or end with the four dots, the ellipses, of nonending to leave room for our fantasy, never broached, of what would happen or be true if we got or were given what we claimed today to want.

If only—the real fantasy being the fantasy of something, anything, finally sufficing, of desire running dry; the fantasy of asking for your own death instead of it coming for you against your will or without your knowledge.

Lu, partner with *Lulai, had it not been for this.* . . . The sentence left unfinished because it is unspeakable and can only be left to intimate what has not come to pass, what has not happened, and therefore cannot be embraced because it is not ours; we fear even imagining its secrets. *Lulai:* the grammar of good fortune, of thankfulness that everything has happened just as it has, of averted catastrophe, the shadow of alternative. The phrase that swiftly and gracefully forces the past into shapes of necessity. *It had to be this way.* This, my life, was destined, sanctioned, cared for by some organizing force. Chaos on the other side of the dots, chaos and the dream, tempting, terrifying, of lives not lived.

But I no longer speak to a God Who I believe shapes the past and will shape the future, Whose word bridges past and future, creates at its utterance the fulfillment of a wish preceding speech. The language I know now is human.

....

Friday morning. Flowers everywhere—in people's arms, in large buckets on the street, on the tables, growing on the trees and bushes; more pedestrians than any other day. The smell of fresh bread; the smell of bitter coffee rising from mugs on crowded tables at cafes. The religious rushing from place to place with packages, conscious all day of Shabbat's nearness; the secular embracing the onset of Israel's short weekends, meandering, browsing in shops, visiting. Soldiers on their way home, guns and kitbags; their cell phones ringing; often it is a mother. People buying up newspapers rapidly, every Israeli taking home at least two or three in yellow and pink plastic bags for the family to read. Buses coming one after the next; travel at its peak. Soon it will be Shabbat.

From my seat at one of Jerusalem's old cafés—there is only one waitress, the menu is only in Hebrew, they seem anyway to serve nothing but iced coffee—I observe, and I write in English. I write a long letter to John, and the paper seems to me the country in which I live, some space between America and Israel; he and I might be its only inhabitants.

I order my coffee awkwardly, a slight exchange, but the sort that instantaneously measures fluency and its absence. It is the sort of exchange that used to bring me pride. I used to wait for such opportunities; now I avoid them.

Hebrew interrupts me now; it disrupts the current of my thought. What I hear comes as a challenge. The demand is translation; each sentence, a new test. To render it precisely, colloquially in English; to capture the tone, the feeling, intention, music. I am no longer able to enjoy what I hear, to participate in and add to it. Instead I save it up. Everything is for the letter. The letter that I am always writing.

When John's letters come—we no longer wait to receive news before we write; our letters cross; we write as if we are having one long conversation—a thin slip announces them. This system makes an event of receipt. I walk to the post office to pick them up, wait in line, see the tellers I have come to know but do not talk to: another example of the silence I keep generally.

Because I cannot wait, I read them walking. *Saadia Gaon, Mitudela, Rambam, Ramban, Keren Kayemet.* These streets now absorb John's stories and phrases. On the balcony where I sit to reread his letters, the slight wind grabs his words, and they go spinning upward in the Jerusalem air. Now he is here. His words mix with the city's words; his breath, his life, has a life here too.

. . . .

In a Jerusalem rose garden, a young man and I, having been introduced to each other by mutual friends, speak to each other in Hebrew; it is his native language. As in the café, as in small shops and bus stations, here too language turns traitor. The sound of my voice floods my ears. I stumble over words, construct sentences in my brain before speaking them aloud. Then they fail.

The man says, in Hebrew, "You speak beautifully."

Frustrated, I reply in English, "I speak terribly. I can never say what I mean."

A sensitive person, he knows that our meeting is uneven. He has come to meet me whole, this meeting only a small excursus from his life, his home, his daily circuits and habits.

Inviting what I have left behind into our meeting, he asks me about my reading. Recommend a book, he says; he likes to read, is interested in what is new and unfamiliar.

I think for a moment, about him, about books; then I suggest
The Mill on the Floss. *He writes down the title in English; then he*
writes down the author's name, George Eliot, in Hebrew.

He tells me he has read Shakespeare and Hardy, but only after
he has closed his little notebook does he tell me that he has read
them in Hebrew.
....

My entire life I had been looking for a lover in Hebrew, it
seemed. I yearned for the romance of that, the mystery and
secrecy. I thought of my grandfather's old letters, archaic and
flowery, language and handwriting both, and my mother telling me how they read like Agnon, the great, classic Hebraist. I
was looking for the lover who could whisper to me in the
language so few Americans know intimately. This would be
the way we would recognize each other. Like Penelope con-
firming Odysseus from his answers to her riddles, riddles easy
enough for the right man, I would know my lover from his
right words, his pleasing, perfect turns of phrase.

From the end of the year I had spent living and studying in
Israel, I was able to anticipate Hebrew forms of speech that
had at first eluded me as a foreigner. I learned to recognize,
then to reproduce, colloquialisms; to hear army slang without
hearing it as slang; to read without a dictionary the newspaper
and contemporary Israeli novels that were notoriously scattered with two Hebrew words combined into one unreadable
lump: *benadam* for *ben adam,* human being; *yomuledet* for *yom*
huledet, birthday. And the hardest words of all, those transliterated from English—*baybiseetehr, tai-dai, Vawtergait*—waiting to
surprise you in their familiarity.

In my first attempts at novel reading I had struggled terribly
just to link the unvocalized letters into words and sensible
grammatical forms. But after the first, second, third novel, I
became able not only to follow the line of the story, but to tell
one character from another by the *sort* of Hebrew their author
had them speaking. One was a working-class family man liv-

ing on the outskirts of Tel Aviv in the late 1950s, accenting his words like an uneducated person, shaming his son with unmeaning tongue; another, a political leftist in today's Jerusalem, accepts proper, speech colorless; a third, a withered old man who had settled with the first pioneers and outlived them, yet had not put aside their mottoes and strangely ordered sentences.

In Israel I listened to the radio's talk shows and popular music. Describing a drunk rock star's debaucheries, the radio host cheerfully announces, *k'tov lev ha-melekh ba-yayin,* כטוב לב המלך ביין: literally, when the king's heart was glad with wine, the king being Ahasuerus of Persia, of the Scroll of Esther, which we read yearly on Purim; I can almost see the dark block letters of the fragile scroll unwound upon a reading table, the congregation listening avidly, children alive for the mention of Haman, gleeful at the downfall of the villain, the silliness of the king. But the radio announcer has no didactic tale or religious ceremony in mind; he talks about Tel Aviv, talks about today.

At the movies I read subtitles not for plot; I understood the plot from the spoken English that entered me without any consciousness on my part, without gratitude or love, like the functioning of a body part that has always functioned. I read subtitles for roots, for brambles, for the strange yet discernible logic of a language's development.

For years after I learned to talk, English had been enough. I practiced it toward mastery. I wanted to say clearly what I meant, to lose the giveaway signs of childhood, the flaws in speech that told adults they might still make choices for me. I came to Hebrew to begin again, to escape the language in which I already knew myself and was known. To return to childhood's struggle for meaning, the slow, desirous swim in and through language; the pleasure of the not-understood and the barely-heard; the glorious intuition that this excess of voices holds secrets, your own and others'.

In this new world I would find my next family, the family in which I was not a child, but myself an adult and parent. I would find someone like myself who belonged and did not belong, who heard all the way to the roots of the words and phrases; heard in sentences the deep punctuation of century and place, the Persia and Ahasuerus of Tel Aviv and rock and roll; the two prophetic words *ben, adam,* of the conglomerate *benadam;* who saw the street sign *Dor, dor, v'dorshav,* דור דור ודרשיו: "each generation and its interpreters" as a helpful marker of location, yet also found himself walking blocks that were pages of psalms, the source of the street's name. I needed a love who could hear without listening but all the same listened.

I found those lovers, and the romance was great. We read and wrote to each other poems and inscriptions, sonnets, quotations in the language of the Jews, ancient, now modern. And the grand, historic words we wove together bore the message, *It is not just your small, fading love.* And they said, *Love is not two people in a room, dying, bones to dust, then nothingness. Love is long lasting, is eternal. Beginning with Adam, love is a human history linking you to your ancestors. Your feet were in Russia, hard wintry ground of the shtetl; your feet were in Babylonia, impressing sand; your feet were at Sinai, the earth burning; your feet were in some garden of Eden, resting for a moment.*

You have been to all these places, and the language you use today, with skill and reverence, proves that you have a past. Your love and your poems remember all those places, and you are not alone. At your wedding communities of people will gather to celebrate survival and endurance, successful transmission and successful inheritance. You will celebrate not yourselves, your names and qualities, but what you come carrying, your bags of knowledge and your bags of obligation— how you cannot leave no matter what you say, no matter what you think or believe. You cannot leave. Your feet are bound.

I do not want a lover in Hebrew anymore. I do not want to love for more than myself. Don't want to speak heavy language. I want

English. Want words you can throw away in the garbage can instead of burying reverently in caves, in earthen vessels, wrapped and shrouded, placed gently in the ground. Don't want words you recite, a martyr meeting your death. "Shema Yisrael Adonai Eloheinu, Adonai Echad": Hear O Israel, the Lord is our God, the Lord is One.

I don't want to hear. I don't want to be called by that name that is not mine, collective, male. I don't want to be herded. I want to live alone and to read, not to hear. I want to live without the commands: Go, come, do, eat, speak, love, choose, burn, tell, keep, do not forget, hear, hear, hear. I have no ears to hear. Not to go, not to do, not to eat, speak, love; to choose something else: the sorry, the wrong, what gets called death; not to burn on the altar, not to keep or be kept but to forget.

To forget.

And later, if I can, to remember. To return. But only when there is sense, when there has been sense-before-sense, and I have chosen to give it up. When chaos no longer looks good and welcoming, hungry for me and I for it; when the world is ready to be put into order; divide, divide, divide. When creation is inevitable.

....

Fall 1996. I have been home from Israel for three months. As my parents' phone calls burst into my quiet Philadelphia home, bringing into my four walls a world that now almost always remains outside, a phone call from New York now does the same. A friend's voice bringing *b'sorot raot*, evil tidings, the news of a tragedy. A young woman from our community has killed herself.

Eight years older than I am, she was a renowned teacher, one of the very first women to teach Talmud in America and Israel's Orthodox institutions. In the circles in which my friends and I travel, everyone knows her by name, if not by face or personally. Many of us have studied with her. But she is not our counterpart precisely; she belongs to a slightly different generation. She and a very few other women paved the way for us to study what we do in the institutions where we do. She came first.

In Manhattan a large synagogue is full to overflowing for this painful funeral. I cannot attend but friends of mine tell me of eulogies and presences. Days later, we continue to call each other, disbelieving still. Years ago, I remember, this woman might have been my roommate had I taken a vacancy that had come up in her apartment.

I would see this woman rarely, but when I did see her, it would be in one of two places: either at the synagogue or walking home from the supermarket, pushing a metal cart with her groceries instead of carrying them all in her arms as I did, always huffing and puffing, needing to stop to rest every ten steps and praying that the handles of the bag did not break before I reached my doorstep. She seemed old to me with her cart, as if she would push it silently into old age.

When I saw her at synagogue, she looked small. She dressed simply, for comfort, as if she did not care greatly what she looked like, but she always looked respectable, never unkempt. If she had not occupied a space in my imagination, I probably would not have seen her. She did not take up much space; she slipped in and out of places. Her reputation for scholarship, brilliance, rarity, stood lonely, without the help of her person.

I never spoke to her, though people encouraged me to. People thought we knew each other, thought we must have known each other. Our interests overlapped, we were serious, we were studious, we were feminists. But I could not speak to her.

On the street and in the synagogue I watched her, and I feared the end I had always feared: loneliness. Invisibility wished for, then violently disavowed. Next to her, I felt large, though I was small; loud, though I was quiet. She was disappearing, and I knew that threat.

I kept myself distinct, as if by such distinction I might protect myself. Her name floated through the city, through Batei

Midrash, through Jewish newspaper articles and journals. Meanwhile, I led a women's prayer group, wrote for a Jewish feminist journal, studied in two central locations, went to the supermarket and the synagogue, yet never did we meet. I did not want to share her *daled amot,* her four cubits, the space of her person, because were we to share it, our names might become one. Then we would be nothing but words: the words we studied, the words others spoke about us. Smoke in the air, with no substance at all.

After her death, dreams visit me, two in a row. While the death of this woman is a tragedy for her friends and her family, for the Jewish people, in my seeing sleep, she belongs only to me. My seeing sleep does not see her.

The first dream takes place in Israel, in Jerusalem. There is a gate and a house. The house belongs to a rabbi who taught me in yeshiva. The first room in the house is filled floor-to-ceiling, wall-to-wall with books. Books and *seforim,* religious texts, both. He has sons, and they run about, wild, with their *kippot* attached to their heads, their *tzitziot* streaming behind them. He has a wife, and she sits in a deep chair, drinking a glass of lemonade; her head is covered by a cotton beret. She is a comfortable sort of woman. The teacher is missing.

In comes A. But it is her dress that I notice. It is short and tightly fitted, and it is black. Its sleeves are tiny, a precious bit of material sliding over the rounds of her shoulders, more alluring than no sleeve at all. Its back is low enough to see the white of her back.

The rabbi enters the room, and he and his wife greet her as if nothing is amiss; the boys too keep running as if no change has occurred. She sits down. The dress pulls against her thighs: I can see her knees and legs. The rabbi introduces us and we smile. My own white skirt, long, full, pleated, brushes against my ankles and my sandals. We are like a portrait of two women painted against a background of books. Yet as she settles into her seat, I rise to leave.

When I dream again, I dream of Yom Kippur. I am sitting in the synagogue next to my sister, holding my *mahzor,* my high holiday prayer book. A. sits a few rows in front of us, alone. I cannot see her face. All I can see is her dress, which is blue and shapeless, its only attempt at grace, a few buttons at the back of the neck. Underneath it, she wears a turtleneck, and she huddles in a bulky wool sweater looking for warmth in the air-conditioned room.

Watching her, I am silent, and though I try to concentrate on prayer, my thought runs in one direction only. *Once she had a body that she cared about, cared about enough to expose, enough to sit in a chair and watch a special dress pull across her small thighs. It was not easy to walk in such a dress, but that did not matter.* While my arms had turned pale and white beneath layers of clothing, her shoulders had felt the heat of the Jerusalem sun. Her fingers tingled in that light.

The dream is short, just this image. A blue dress instead of a black one, chill instead of heat, late fall for summer. In dreams we pass each other as shadows again, she in her dresses, I in mine. We pass each other on the Sabbath and on Yom Kippur, among the prayer shawls and prayer books, the knees and legs, the words and fabrics. Only she is no longer living.

I knew she was disappearing.

....

A few months after the suicide, my friend Ruth calls to invite me back to the women's prayer service I helped to found but no longer attend. She tells me she has invited a scholar-in-residence, one of the earliest proponents of a feminist Orthodoxy. I am reluctant to go. I do not want to see in the younger women's faces any hint of my past. I imagine that although almost ten years have elapsed since I was in their shoes, they will be fighting the battles I fought in my college years, with no signs of progress.

Yet when I arrive, I see that the Beit Midrash has been transformed. Once it was a bare room lined with books, crowded with tables, decorated only by two curtains: the graying, frayed *mehitza* and the dark, embroidered *parokhet,* the covering before the Ark.

The shadows of men's bodies hover everywhere. Their rounded backs as they stare into the mirror of the Gemara's pages, the record of their weight upon the woven chairs, their fingerprints on the *yad,* the pointer that touches the Torah scroll so that human hands do not. Open windows where they have left them open, bookmarks in books, calendars of participation: who will *leyn* the Torah portion, who will be called to the Torah to recite its blessings, who will teach the daily lesson after services, who will reorder the books after study, who will collect the charity, and who will call the names of the ill.

The only women's names are the names of the ill: the female ill and the mothers of the male ill.

Women's shadows hover too in this Beit Midrash: the sweep of long skirts, the tread of sneakers. When these students show up in my classes, recognizable by their dress, I look at them with the goal of forgetting what I know. I try not to recognize that they rush out at the end of class because they want to be on time to afternoon prayer. I like to imagine that they are strangers to me, as I am a stranger to them. I like to pretend that I don't know what they eat and sing, what their homes look like, the cycle of their year, the rhythm of their day. I play America with them: the mystery of someone else's origins, the difference of the individual.

But tonight in the Beit Midrash I try to set aside my prejudices and assumptions. The Sabbath is coming, and tall candles stand on the window sills, enough pairs of candles for all the women to light. Flames flicker in the glass of the windows, and I see fire against the outside, fire against the trees and wind and darkening air, blue turning orange turning dusk, then black, then blue again. The tables have been removed. There are fifteen chairs set in a semicircle. There are flowers at the door: lilies—peach, orange, and white. Lilies beside the books.

Women enter one and two at a time, and they are wearing short skirts and long. They are wearing pants, and one woman comes from the gym in shorts. Two women come with book bags. Most come with hair still wet: the rush toward the sabbath. This group looks different than the groups I have known. Many of the women seem to know each other; they greet each other happily.

Ruth begins to lead our prayer. Her eyes are closed as she prays and her twenty-year-old body sways. I hold my prayer book, forgetting to turn the pages. I am absorbed in her prayer.

The voice: I had forgotten the voice. Ruth's voice is full of song. Birds are in the room, and instead of night, it is day. The sun high above: her youth. Her voice slides into dusk, lowers itself. We sing without words, a new melody for *L'kha Dodi:* "Let us go, my love, and greet the Sabbath bride." Now we dance, a circle of hands and feet and eyes. The Sabbath queen is invisible, as she is meant to be. Like Elijah, like Moses, like all the spirits and the angels, the queen is here and missing.

When the dance and song come to their end and the service to its end, Ruth invites the older woman to speak; Ruth has just begun to date her son.

The woman-scholar stands up and in this private space offers us the easiest of histories, personal and didactic at once. From origin to redemption, a story of salvation. *This is how it was for me. I found friends; we wanted to pray; we wanted to hold the Torah; we asked the rabbi. We began to gather once a month. Twenty-five years later, we still gather once a month in the very same room.*

A lecturer now myself, I recognize that this woman has evaded the teacher's tax to the student: the honor of preparation. She speaks with a ready answer for every question. She finds ease in just being herself.

The young women would like to believe her. They would like her to be timeless and wise, a sphinx, an oracle, anything, so long as there is something.

And so they ask her questions. The Orthodox young women ask, will women one day read from the Torah before men? Will the books and legal opinions of women bind? Will a woman someday, perhaps within our lifetimes, be named rabbi?

They are asking *eyn-sof* questions, endless questions, for which there are no words, let alone answers in preparation. The room is filled with the sound of language that merely hums but does not divide. My own ears take in the buzz and hum, wait for something sharper. It comes.

When the young girl asks, "Will women ever lead men in prayer? Will we ever pray together?" the older woman says, *"Think of it this way. It's the men's sorrow that they can't hear our beautiful voices raised in prayer."*

Those are the words I have been waiting for. The formulation has been impossible to expect, but I recognize it when I hear it. These are the words, and the tone, that tell me I no longer belong. . . . .

At home, alone after the service, I wonder to myself what *the men's sorrow* means to the college women, those participants younger than myself by seven years, eight years. When I ask Ruth a few days later what she thought of it all, she says, "Oh, I don't buy that." She doesn't buy it and it disturbs her, yet it is not decisive for her. It doesn't bring her suffering. Can this be solely a matter of temperament?

Two months later, Ruth tells me that students are organizing a large conference at Yale University on "Women and Judaism." When she tells me, I assume she means it is a conference for Orthodox women. At times it seems to me (absurdly, I know), that other Jewish women are living in the Promised Land: what could they possibly have to discuss or plan or improve? No, Ruth corrects me; it is not particular to Orthodox women. It is open to all Jewish college women and any other interested parties. Panels and activities will treat such subjects as women in the Middle East peace movement, the representation of women in Talmudic texts, contemporary Jewish women's art, the laws and customs of baking challah, lesbian Jewish life, Jewish women's literature, a newly developing Jewish women's archive, the problem of battered Jewish women in America, and yes, there will also be sessions on concerns unique to Orthodox women. Do I want to come?

I do want to come—I am fascinated by the scope of the conference and its hundreds of preregistered attendees—but I know I will be terribly lonely among all these vibrant young women. When I was their age, nineteen, twenty, twenty-one, my friends and I were not planning or attending conferences with other Jewish women in our free time, it occurs to me. We were going to weddings.

Weddings were what brought us together in celebration, again and again. In order to dance together in a circle, to sing with joy, we needed a real live bride in the center, not the intangible bride of the Sabbath around whom Ruth and her friends had danced in the Beit Midrash. It was as if alone, young single women, we had nothing of our own to celebrate, only things to fight for. Like wallflowers at a prom, we could not imagine dancing alone, breaking into the center of the room, making something beautiful of what seemed a shame or embarrassment.

The dark dresses of the bridesmaid hung in my closet and those of my nearest friends as ghostly warnings; the shoes stood stock still, worn once, hastily stepped out of. The vacancy and droopiness of those dresses: these were our dark futures. Victorian literature made as much sense as it did to me because I understood the notion of spinsterhood at twenty-three.

By the time I was twenty-five, I had been to more than thirty weddings, had been a bridesmaid six times.

This was the sum of Binah. The girls who had tried for a year to sit, to learn in yeshiva: they (we) had learned well the lessons of the kitchen and the bedrooms converted into a makeshift Beit Midrash. There *was* no Beit Midrash in our futures; there was no true sitting allowed. What really awaited us after the single year devoted to study was a book while standing in the kitchen, a quick glance at words before bed.

If not that, we could choose aloneness. We could have our tempting, smooth table and our lovely, heavy books. We could have the famous room of one's own. But if we chose that, then, as Virginia Woolf had *not* specified, not having been to yeshiva, there would be no celebration for us. The room of my own, a studio apartment, would have to be enough. It would have to be enough to have that room and to know that somewhere else, another woman, maybe another two or three women, had their single rooms. Famine was back.

What was it, I wondered, that allowed Ruth and her friends, her compatriots, to dance with all the confidence in the world? How did they dare to dance lacking the stiff and billowing white dress, the princess shoes, the sheer veil, the delicate flowers woven in the hair? What had they learned that I had not? What had they rejected that I had accepted?
. . . .
For days I consider these questions, this difference. I know that like me, Ruth has been to many weddings. It is not as if the life of tradition—the custom of early weddings and young motherhood—has disappeared just because a small circle of women can dance together joyously or even because hundreds of young women can gather at Yale University without men watching. In fact, I know that Ruth likes to imagine her own wedding, that she sees herself as a future wife and mother. Yet I also know that she can imagine sitting. She can imagine both things. Her womanly future is not an image of aloneness. She

imagines sitting *and* moving from room to room. She actually imagines dancing, a thing I love to do.

The difference between Ruth and me is only a few years. I was born in 1970; she was born in 1977. More to the point, I graduated from high school in 1988 and studied in Israel in 1989. When I went to Israel to learn, the girls' program at Brovender's was in its third year of existence. My friends and I were the first girls from Chicago ever to attend. And we had never studied Talmud because our yeshiva high school did not teach it to girls. In 1988 there were two centers in Jerusalem that offered young women, precollege women, intensive training in Talmud. Neither of them was more than two years old.

When we returned to the United States, the culture of women's learning was seriously limited. The extraordinary Drisha Institute for Jewish Education, New York's only center for women's higher learning of classical Jewish texts, had been founded in 1979, ten years earlier, but when you arrived there to study, you found folding tables and bad light. The floors were concrete and the windows were dirty; there was certainly no open Beit Midrash in which women learned in pairs, daily and regularly. The *shiurim,* or classes, that I took were excellent; the other women students, who ranged in age from twenty to eighty, were also excellent. That should have been all that mattered, but it was not. How can we get more women to come learn, Drisha's founder asked me and a few of my friends. It was partially a matter of consciousness, of knowing the option existed. Women did not know.

By the time Ruth finished high school, a girl had to compete to get into what had been Brovender's and was now known as Midreshet Lindenbaum. The number of women enrolled yearly had jumped from sixty to over one hundred. In 1996 the school's old apartment buildings were abandoned, and a full campus was planned and built in northeastern Jerusalem. The program in which I had studied was into its tenth year, and at least two more *mikhlalot,* founded between 1988 and 1990, offered their students training in Talmud. My own high school in Chicago had made Talmud a voluntary part of any girl's education. Drisha had collected the funds for a beautiful Beit Midrash of its own, with a small cadre of full-time fellowship women learning all day. Child care was available. Planning for a girls' high school program was underway. And many Manhattan women of all ages knew the institution by name.

These changes did not mean that the lay of the land was entirely different: of course it wasn't. Public perception changes slowly, Orthodox rabbinic predispositions and dicta even more slowly. But it was enough to make a person hopeful. It was enough to suggest that a group of young women could dance for the sheer joy of the Sabbath and the Torah without a girl-bride at the center.

In April I go to the conference with Ruth and her friends, and I can see that it is an extraordinary event. But I feel like a much older sister at the younger sister's slumber party. There are only a handful of women my age present since most twenty-six-year-olds have full-time jobs or burgeoning careers; almost all my friends have their own families and homes to tend too.

I am neither here nor there. A doctoral candidate, I am not fully a professional, but I am not entirely a student either. Partnered but not married, I am secretly alone and secretly befriended. A friend's four-year-old son has asked me where my children are, and when I answer that I don't have any, he asks me where my parents are. I see his point.

....

When I was five, six, seven years old, sitting next to my mother in synagogue, following her finger, following the words, she would say, "In France and Israel and Africa, all over the world, Jews are reading the same story today. If you were in any of those places, Lanaleh, you could find your way."

I have lost the line. Now that I no longer go to the synagogue on the Sabbath nor read aloud the weekly Torah portion that

Jews all over the world read in a shared, regular cycle, I no longer know what week it is.

Though I still pray almost every day, some months Rosh Hodesh, the days of the new moon and Hebrew month, pass me by unaware because I was not in synagogue to hear their date announced in advance. I forget to include the appropriate prayers and treat it as an ordinary day instead of a small holiday. I have dreams regularly of eating on Yom Kippur, the holiest day of the Jewish year, the day that even the most assimilated of Jews come to synagogue, beat their breasts, and fast. In my dreams I have woken up alone in John's bed and forgotten that I am fasting. I drink water; I eat cereal with milk, begin to drink a tall glass of orange juice, and all of a sudden, I drop the glass. It cracks on the floor as I wake up. It is not Yom Kippur. But similar things do happen now.

Once I woke up on Shabbat and prepared to make coffee for John and me. I walked into the darkened kitchen and took out two mugs. Because it was Shabbat and I observed the prohibition against cooking, I had filled an urn of hot water that would stay plugged in throughout the night and day, as many observant Jews do. I put a spoonful of coffee in a mug—no grinding of fresh beans on Shabbat—and then began to add hot water from the urn to the coffee. Immediately, as the stream hit the coffee grounds and they began to liquefy, I gasped and removed my finger from the tap instantaneously.

By Jewish legal standards I had just "cooked" the coffee, thus desecrating Shabbat by performing one of the thirty-nine prohibited creative acts. What I should have done was to pour the hot water into one mug, then pour it into another mug, then add the coffee. This method insures that the water is no longer at a temperature that can "cook" anything, according to the legal definition of cooking.

At this moment, John asleep in my room, me aghast with a cup of coffee in my hand, I know that my life has ceased to be intelligible to most, if not all, Jews who share the minute yet fundamental concerns of cooking on the Sabbath. Before the seeking faithful, those who wake up each morning to serve God their Creator, who strive to keep all the laws, even those inconvenient and demanding, I stand in a kind of shame born of past community. I know what once I would have thought of myself.

Toward the others, the mass of easy, assured Orthodox Jews, I feel the unpleasant emotions of anger and spite; this group of Jews reminds me quite suddenly of the leisurely, well-fed Christians of pre-evangelical England. If the censorious majority that George Eliot calls "the world's wife" knew about my life, it would reject me because I have stepped outside the circle of acceptable transgressions.

This circle, invisible and undescribed, is nonetheless familiar to most modern Orthodox Jews of the same generation and perhaps their parents too. Is there a religious system that does not have some such mechanism? Now, in 1997, the circle drawn by Gen-X modern Orthodox American Jews tolerates bending the laws of Shabbat and kashrut (dietary laws) for participation in the wider world; it features forebearance toward casual observance and nonobservance of the obligations of prayer and blessing; it allows for a complete willingness to forget the call to study Torah; and it bounces back flexibly when hungry young Jews silently engage in all things sexual with each other, so long as there is no result.

Yet the circle is finally a circle; it keeps its secrets within. It does not allow for overlap with any other circle. *Goyim* are *goyim*.

If people (Jews) knew about my private life, they would blame me. But wouldn't they also blame feminism? Feminism and jeans, English literature, excessive education: these things, coming from the outside, have ruined me.

How much easier it would all be if we were talking about the casual transgression of Jewish law. If I were simply lax, all things could later be forgiven; forgotten too. Observant Jews believe in *t'shuvah,* honest return. Honest return to the belief in rabbinic authority

But is not the real sin overenthusiasm, my having cared too much? It has never been the masses of women who do not pray that the rabbis find worthy of fearful rebuke; it is women who want to pray publicly, who want to *pray,* that cause trouble. Male zealousness can be troubling to authority, yes, but female zealousness for anything is always seen as zealousness for being female.

I have stepped outside the circle, and yet outside is nowhere good. John certainly isn't there. After I exclaim over the coffee, he drinks my cup. Not because he wants to enjoy a transgression; that would mean the existential categories lived for him. If he were to enjoy the sin, then we'd be talking.

Later, in his own apartment, he will improve upon this first cup by grinding fresh beans, then boiling cold, fresh water. He'll make himself a cup of weekend coffee, perhaps bike into town to pick up a fresh croissant to eat with it. I will not bike with him. Fairly often, he calls on Saturday. His memory fails. Weekend is one undistinguished span for him; Saturday and Sunday are both days of rest. He calls and talks into the machine, knowing I am home. He waits for me to grant him the lover's privilege of picking up when I will speak to no one else. Then he remembers it is Saturday, and I hear his voice change. It fills with surprise and knowledge as his conversation moves from being addressed to me to being addressed to himself. *Of course,* he says, impatient with himself, *it's the Sabbath; of course you won't answer.*

It is an idea of time that separates us, but it separates us fully. One weekend, college friends of his come to visit. We eat dinner together at my house on Friday night, and then they set out for a party across town. When I explain that I don't drive or ride in cars on the Sabbath, one of them jokes,

"Well, we could tie you to the back of the car and drag you, couldn't we?"

Circles and circles. There is a violence here.

Yet even in the absence of violence, in the presence of love, aloneness feels often like abandonment. When John shows me how unnatural he still finds the order according to which I live, it seems to me he has forgotten not the day or the custom, but me.

. . . .

In spring, we read together still. But when summer arrives with its murky, Philadelphia heat (a year ago I was in Israel, the coolness of Jerusalem evenings and its stone), I know I will move to New York City to write my dissertation. I will write chapters about a pattern I have noticed in mid-Victorian fiction: the theft of precious objects and their replacement with the priceless value of fellow-feeling and human sympathy.

I saw it first in Eliot's *Romola:* a Renaissance library of rare and unique manuscripts, gems, and sculpted busts is dispersed and sold by a perfidious husband and son-in-law. Then, chapters later, the money from the sale already forgotten by the reader, it resurfaces to be exchanged for food by Romola, the self-renouncing wife and daughter. With it she feeds her husband's bastard children, adopted as her own. Precious objects lost, a collection dismantled; even more precious human life sustained, a community built. Yet the great novelist that George Eliot is, the loss of the texts copied by the father's hand remains a tragedy of the novel. A library divided, its benefits transformed: a tragedy and a redemption all in one. How much there is to write here.

I will write it in New York. I want also to seek a new Jewish community, perhaps not Orthodox, perhaps egalitarian. If I cannot make a decisive break with the Jewish world and must make instead the break with a man I love and if at the same time I cannot make a satisfying pact with the

Orthodox community I come from, then my only choice is to make a new circle.

....

The summer wanes and the move nears. When I consider packing, emptying the home I have made myself for the last three years, I find myself overcome by all I own. I look about the apartment, not knowing what to bring and what to leave. John advises me to take everything, not to make choices now, when I cannot yet see my future, but to make them when I have reached my destination, when I am living in my present. He helps me learn to pack haphazardly.

We pack the books together too. At his instructions, we organize them by size and height and width rather than content. Suddenly all the books are one. The tall volumes of Gemara fit perfectly in the box stacked with Vintage International paperbacks, and my cheap Bantam editions of George Eliot's novels are held in place by the stiff bindings of two thick Passover Haggadot. When I arrive in New York alone, the sorting will begin, but for now, in the darkness of the boxes, all the books will rest together, against each other.

The day of the move, late June, I awake beside John. I have barely slept. Movers arrive almost immediately, and within an hour and a half, everything I own is in their truck. John kisses me good-bye for now. "Nothing is irrevocable," he tells me when he sees the tears in my eyes; it is not a death, just a parting; it is not a parting of the Old World, just a train ride between cities. Nothing is irrevocable, and yet, suddenly, nothing is the same. All the change I have wanted: it is mine.

Not enough time has elapsed, I think to myself upon arriving in New York. Changes in destiny should be slower, should involve long journeys across oceans, time for the soul to catch up with the body, time for the heart to reinvent itself. I have packed the last of my boxes this very morning, and now, merely four hours later, I must disinter what I have hidden.

Still, as I begin to cut through the tape, open the flaps of the first box, then the second, mysterious too, I find this modern unpacking bears all the tenderness of lifting half-forgotten yet intensely loved things from a chest whose contents you have not seen for months or years. In part, this is because I have not packed all the boxes myself. John's hands last touched some of these things.

Here is the fragile purple blown-glass vase my father bought me in Israel, with yellow roses, I was eight; here are my CDs, and here the telephone. Here is my high school yearbook; I didn't remember having that in Philadelphia; all this time I had thought it was in Chicago. Here is a stray photo, Jonathan dressed up as Snoopy for a play we wrote one summer; another, Naomi on her first day of school; she insisted on wearing her white winter boots though it was August.

By evening my books are on their shelves, my clothing is unpacked, my bed is made, and my plants are on the windowsill. Still, strangeness overwhelms me. In the morning I lived in Philadelphia. I wrote at my desk early in the day and walked to the library in the afternoons. In the early evenings I made my way to John's, and we sat on the porch and drank cool gin and tonics; I ate the limes for both of us. Late at night, in the summer heat, we returned to the porch, sat quietly, end of day.

Twelve hours later, and that is all a thing of the past. Though I lie on the same sheets and pillows that I lay on last night—they smell faintly of John, of summer sweat, of my perfume and my old apartment—eventually those light threads will disintegrate and be gone. I will bring the cartons down to the basement for recycling, and it will seem as if what is, always was.

....

When I was ten and my father's father died, cartons surrounded us. Cartons holding books, a library. We buried my grandfather in the ground but kept the books above ground. We buried my grandfather saying, Dust to dust; saying, God gave and took, let His name be blest, but we packed his books in cartons. My father took eight boxes, my aunt took two, my grandmother four; the rest remained in Ann Arbor, a bequest to the University of Michigan.

At home, in our house, the books stayed in their cartons, stacked neatly in the basement, next to the softly bagged and boxed Wedgewood dishes we used once a year, on Passover; next to the cartons holding my mother's books from college, old papers of my father's, paperback novels: things we needed to keep but not to use.

The cartons accumulated dust; they took on the shape of their surrounding constraints; they settled against the walls, the floor, themselves. Until, one day, I opened a box, and then another, to discover books frail as my grandfather had been the last time I saw him. Yellow pages, brittle, cracking upon the slightest touch. The books said, Don't open us, we cannot bear it. Keep us from the light, keep us from use and life; the last hands that touched us were not yours.

I lift one book from the box, then a second and a third. There is nowhere to set them down since many of them are holy books: the Bible, volumes of the Talmud, commentaries of Rashi, Nahmanides, and ibn Ezra, writings of Saadia Gaon, Rav Hai Gaon, Rav Shrira Gaon. Mesilat Yesharim, Hovat Ha'Levavot, Sefat Emet, Orot Ha-Kodesh: the Path of the Righteous, the Duty of Hearts, the Language of Truth, Lights of Holiness. Torah Temimah, Midrash Rabbah, Yalqut Shimoni. Then the tools of the scholar's trade: Cassuto, the Anchor Bible, Mandelkorn's concordance, Jastrow's dictionary, Even-Shoshan's too; Weingreen's scholarly Hebrew grammar and Gesenius'. Red spines, black, brown, forest green, some taped and fortified.

Faint pencil marks, translations into Greek and Arabic, underlinings, question marks, abbreviated notes to the self: of source, parallel passages, deviations from other versions. A name and a date, counting from Creation.

My grandfather and I meet for a moment in the basement, beside the cartons, by the books. Souls without bodies, we meet to talk the way the sages traversed generations, years and centuries slipping away in the search after correct interpretation. In school I could never remember if Rashi knew the rabbis of the Talmud. The eleventh century and the fifth: they all came before me.

Down the stairs comes my father to discover the boxes finally disturbed. He helps me balance the books in stacks. I hand him volume after volume.

1922, 1928, 1929; 5682, 5688, 5689.

Precious, broken, old, old books: these books are first and second tablets too. Signs of sin and insurrection, the forgotten and the lost, they are, nonetheless, beloved beyond the first.

Tree, Light, Fruit

Ann Arbor, 2005

We're into new books now, books of a different sort. All have pictures. Some are made of paper, others of cloth and plastic and cardboard. Books for eating as well as reading.

When I go into the bookstore now—Afterwords, on Main Street—I head for the back room, where it's all pleasure. There's a rug on the floor and three tall bookcases, two blue tables, a few turning racks. "Children," the sign above the door says, and that is true, but the sign should say "Parents" as well. When you go to the area actually marked "Parents," you find books on breast feeding, how to deal with the unruly child, how to manage sibling rivalry, feng shui and yoga for your baby. I skip the adult books for the room with all the surprises, the ideas and things you want to see, hear, touch, taste, smell, fall asleep remembering.

No one questions the right of the mother to choose books for her chid. Perhaps no one thinks of it. Such a quiet thing, private even when it's public, of minimal consequence when compared to other matters. No one watches, and you build a little world.

In a few months we will start going to the library. By then Priya will walk steadily among bookcases; she will know how to balance herself, to stand and hold things at the same time; she will learn to look forward to story hour among the bean bags and puppets. Then we will borrow books for a week at a time, sit on the cushions at the library and browse books together, share books with other children and parents, get a library card. For now, though, our library is at home.

I buy books with an abandon I have only in the sphere of books. I hold off on clothing and toys and decorations, which others, too, love to buy and make. When Priya was born, she received an abundance of tiny, lovely girl clothes in soft pink and deep teal, vivid purple, pristine white, tender yellow. Hats, dresses, one-piece suits, blankets, the softest materials imaginable. I loved to handle these things, even to launder them and then lay them on the plastic rack, avoiding the dryer for fear they would shrink to be even smaller than they started out. Those clothes now look tiny next to her growing body. Now, a year later, her clothes are mostly beautiful hand-me-downs from her cousins, my brother's girls, Jessica and Emily. Her many toys—musical instruments, sorting bins, blocks, animals, dolls, puzzles, rattles—have all come as gifts. The decorations in her room—hot air ballooons hanging from the ceiling, papier-mâché globes with tiny baskets and strings, clouds of puffy cotton, one globe designed with her initials, another with the Mona Lisa, another half-moon and stars on one side and sun and sky on the other—these were her father's project and gift. That leaves for me . . . diapers and books.

. . . .

I think I never wanted to dwell too much on the prospect of buying books for a child of my own because the doubt as to whether it would ever come to pass—the finding of a mate, the great blessing of conception, healthy pregnancy, successful delivery—all seemed so much to hope for, just as much to be deprived of. Now that Priya is nearly one, I can testify that of all the joys of being her mother, one of the greatest is looking at her, listening to her, and then finding the right books.

. . . .

I was pregnant for thirty-eight weeks with an unknown, unknowable being. I didn't want to know its sex, and Ori let me decide since he was not sure whether he wanted to know. The ultrasound at twenty weeks upset me. Too technical, too much information. It was fine for me that the doctor know; that was her business. It was right to check to see whether the developing being was healthy and well. But I did not want to see on the outside—on a screen, no less—what was inside me and secret: a gift, an invasion, a stowaway, changing every moment, growing parts and abilities, resting when I was at motion, moving when I was at rest. I felt strongly about it: bringing this proto-child from dark into light seemed to me like pulling a plant from the ground to check its roots. The technician measured head circumference, the length of the femur and the tibia; he noted the already distinguishable four chambers of the heart. It was extraordinary, what they could do and see on a computer and then print for us. It was extraordinary and I was grateful, but I really disliked it. What I liked was sitting on the table in my doctor's quiet office, Ori at my side, and listening to the heartbeat of our growing baby fill the room. So fast, so strong, so regular, so loud!

I liked listening to the heartbeat because it felt unintrusive. There was no image to match the sound, no "catching" of the fetus, just a being-with, our own momentary capacity to hear a rush and a beat that we knew was constant and repeating. It kept me company, this rush and beat; it measured time inside me, week after week. The heartbeat was life, sure life; animal confidence; the regularity and generosity of day and night; week, month, year; the seasons; parent, grandparent, child; year, decade, century; Old World and New; one language and another. It measured all the divides and all the gradations, one thing easing into another, silence and sound merging, life and nonlife less separate than I had thought, this being without a name.

. . . .

Ori is a doctoral candidate in literature, and I am now an assistant professor. I have done what I set out to do: I wrote a dissertation and got a job. In 2001 I left New York and the East Coast for Michigan, where I teach English literature and Jewish

Studies, courses in Bible and Midrash alternating with courses on the history of the novel, Victorian ethics and economics.

John teaches at Harvard and occasionally he and my sister meet for coffee or take in a movie in Somerville, where she lives and works. All but one of my grandparents has died. My brother has three children now, two girls and one boy, Will, who was born a month before Priya.

I met Ori at a party. It was held in Huntington, New York. Good friends were moving away to California, and I had missed their son's bris; it had followed immediately on the heels of my bubbi's death. The snowy, ice days of 2000; everything was frozen and there was an entire apartment to sort and clean with my mother and sister. Diplomas to find; old gowns and hats to try on and then parcel out—this to the thrift shop in the Village, this home with me; papers to discover, the bills for the living room furniture, written out in the beautiful longhand of a time gone by; the bill for my mother's wedding dress; my mother's birth announcements, a little pink bow on each aged vanilla card. I could not go to Huntington for a bris that February. We were in the throes of death. Births were long-ago things, lives already unfolded.

Five months later, in late spring, the friends who held the bris invite me to their going-away party; they are moving to California. Alan is a Reform rabbi; Shara is my old friend from Barnard, now a graduate student in Comparative Religion at Columbia. They arrange a ride for me with a friend of Alan's, another young rabbi, good-looking, amiable, single. I wonder when I get in the car whether they are suggesting something: a *shidduch,* a match. Immediately, though, I know this is no match for me. A nice guy, but who would have guessed he was a rabbi? He wore high-top sneakers and Bermuda shorts, listened intently to the ballgame as we drove. As we made our way to Huntington, he told me he was going to begin a new regimen in which he would make sure to study Torah at least twenty minutes a day since he had discovered that so much of his time was taken up with synagogue business, the board, religious school development, new building plans.

He wasn't Orthodox; that was the problem, I thought to myself. But was I? Can a woman consider herself Orthodox when she has loved a man who is not Jewish? When she has thought of a life outside the laws of purity, sexual and otherwise? I did not have illusions about my piety. But I didn't have illusions about his either. The daily work of this rabbi was not in the world of Torah study, nor the world of silent good deeds or unacclaimed teaching or even the vital, silent tasks that allow for the other tasks: setting up chairs in the synagogue, setting out prayer books.

You could say that this had nothing to do with denomination, with Reform or Orthodox, Conservative or Reconstructionist, but was simply a matter of sensibility. Here was a man who was attracted to the world of money and power, the ins and outs of an institutional life that put him at the center. He was also attracted to Judaism. You could say that many Orthodox rabbis come to the rabbinate in the same indirect way.

This would be true. And yet what was missing in him, what was missing in so many non-Orthodox Jewish men, rabbis and otherwise, that I had met in the four years between John and Ori, was the conviction that had been written out on a tattered sign hanging in the Beit Midrash in my high school: *da lifnei mi atah omed,* דע לפני מי אתה עומד. Know before whom you stand.

Countless synagogues worldwide bear this lesson, this truth—in their sanctuaries, before the Ark, above the Eternal Light, on the walls. *Know before whom you stand.* So little explained and so much implied. Your plans for a building, for a religious school, for a citywide project: keep them in perspective. Know to whom you owe your life, your capacity for breath and basketball. Keep it always in your mind. Before you take a bite of an apple, say a blessing. After you use the bathroom, say a blessing. When you see a disabled person or an extraordinarily beautiful one or a flash of lightning or when you have escaped a dangerous situation unharmed, acknowledge the source of it all through blessing. Never let a holiday or a Jewish date take you by surprise. Live by the calendar of faith, of an ancient people. On this calender it is a period of mourning or a time of counting or a month of joy or a harvest interval, not July or May or March or October. Is your birthday in April, or does it find its definition in relation to Passover? What is real and what is a half-belief? Are you in the gym for an hour a day and the Beit Midrash for twenty minutes? Or when you have eighty minutes, do most of them find you in the Beit Midrash?

This is strict. Perhaps it even seems unrealistic or fantastic, especially in America. But having lived that way for years, I knew the difference. It wasn't the difference between Orthodox and not-Orthodox, after all. Simply "being Orthodox" did not in any way mean that you lived confronted by the truth of *da lifnei mi atah omed;* you could be Orthodox in your practice and never for a moment be struck by the gravity of your place in the world. But even if being Orthodox did not entail recognizing *da lifnei mi atah omed,* those who *did* recognize it were almost always Orthodox. As a consequence. If you were fully, constantly aware of the One before Whom you stood, wouldn't you too try to build a life whose every detail reflected that understanding?

At the turn of the century in New York City the truth on the ground was that those who lived with this knowledge almost all chose a way of life that an observer would have identified as Orthodox. There were exceptions among Jewish men of other denominations, but in my experience they were extraordinarily rare. So there I was, in Huntington, with a rabbi who was not nearly pious enough for me: me, a woman who had done a thing much graver than devoting more time to basketball than learning.

And there, in Huntington, I met a different man. Not pious but something else, something undefined, something attractive, magnetic, but not pious. I couldn't have evoked him in advance, couldn't place him even after we had talked all afternoon, couldn't place him later. He was no *yeled tov Y'rushalayim*, a "good Jerusalem boy," a perfectly sincere Jewish childman. He did not feed my Jacob fantasies; he did not draw all the synagogue light to him so that there was none left in which I might stand. He frustrated my categories. I would not have known how to write him.

There, at the party, he sat on the couch, keeping up his end of a conversation that looked to be lagging. A woman had just walked into the room: she was a pretty blonde. She walked straight toward the rabbi who had given me a ride; she was his fiancée. My friend Shara cradled her son to nurse him while her husband leaned over her shoulder, singing to him. Not yet knowing his name, I moved across the room toward Ori.

....

We got married in 2002. When I think of Ori, a George Eliot word comes to mind: ardent. A word that means both passion and earnestness. Both the sudden, immediate, impulsive spirit of giving and generously taking from a beloved intimate and the watchful, philosophical nature that thinks to alleviate the pain it detects in the world at large.

Ardent: the Daniel Derondas and Dorotheas. The Maggie Tullivers and Felix Holts. Yet Ori and I are modern Jews, not mid-nineteenth-century evangelically inclined British Christians, agnostics, foundlings, writers. Ori grew up within Reform Judaism. He found things and people of value there, but he could not find enough books. He could not find rabbis who followed primarily in the rabbinic tradition of scholarship and lives of learning.

He wants a table spread with heavy books, all of them open at once. He has an image of himself before that table: the owner of hands that know immediately where to turn. He has an image of himself teaching: students and children both.

Well before we marry, rather soon after we have begun to date, we argue about where our hypothetical children will go to school. The table with books is set in our home, but what if we send our children to public school? Will they learn to read what we want them to read? What if we send them to Orthodox yeshiva? Will they live in the world we want for them? What about Conservative day school? Then what about *kashrut*? What about *mikveh*? What about all the laws that separate Jews from non-Jews?

Also before we marry he tells me he has an image of a child wrapped warm in his tallis, held against his body, as he prays in the synagogue.

Ori is not an Orthodox Jew in terms of his belief or his relationship to ritual. The word "spirit" is not part of his lexicon; he can talk about the spirit in which Maimonides believes or the spirit that Genesis describes; he has studied these texts in university and on his own. But he does not believe he himself has a soul or spirit. The dead are fully dead to him. Traditional Jewish practice *is* meaningful to him but not because God asks it of him; he elects it.

From the time I was a child, I remember hearing people say approvingly that Judaism was not a religion of faith but of practice. It is Christianity, I hear, that requires daily recitation of catechisms, that works at thought control, that judges you based on intention as much as action, that needs you to believe in all you do, as you do it. Judaism says, "Do it, and you will come to do it for the right reasons." No one will ask you what you believe or what you *mean* if you come to the synagogue to pray. This system, I see even as a child, could mean a life of doing it, all on the slender provision that some day intention and action will coalesce. That meaning will come spilling out of duty and obligation.

The letter of law and the spirit. Jesus Christ covered up under sheets as I learned to read Hebrew, learned my first pages of Torah, ate the sweet kosher cookies that were not the body but the letters themselves. Ori is the letter. But he is so in more ways than one, as words mean more things than one. He is the letter in loving the letters of the law and its words and sentences and poetry. He is also its letter in carrying out many of its practices with me. He is the letter in questioning the spirit and in so doing, creating the spirit.

Aesthetics or psychological comfort or sheer habit should not, Ori says to me one night, justify a life. When he says this to me, it's like being told, "Judaism is a religion of faith, not practice." He's turned it upside down. The fact that we like how things sound or taste or how the week feels when Shabbat comes to crown it: these facts are not enough. They are not guilty confessions, mind you—there is no prohibition on enjoyment, no correspondent drop in the value of the enjoyed deed or word—but they are not enough.

I agree. It would be a terrible thing to live a life of faithless practice or narcissistic practice. Shouldn't it be that the Golden Calf of Practice sustains you only through the times of difficulty, whether that means a period of crisis or simply a period when the demands of living are so intense that time eludes you to contemplate what you are about? But what, then, is the relation between practice and faith? Between what we do and what we feel and think, and think we know?

Maybe the truest version of the relation comes out at the oddest, least convenient moments when your child asks you, "Why this? Why not that?" Is it God you immediately find yourself speaking of? Or your grandmother and her *shabbos* candlesticks? Is it the Holocaust of European Jewry? Or Hebrew, the ancient, now modern language of the Jews? Is it the

miraculous victories of the Israel of 1967? The difficult com-
promises of Israel in the early twenty-first century? The vision
of your own, imagined great-grandchildren? The weight of old
books and fragile scrolls? The smell of the *etrog* (citron), the
feel of *tefillin* (phylacteries)? The natural world, in all its might
and glory?

What do I say when Priya asks, "Why do we say Shema at
night? Why do we kiss a *siddur* when it drops? And why can't I
play the piano on Shabbat?"

How can I answer her in a good, strong sentence? It would
be hard for me to say, using the digestible, familiar, parent-
like term for God, "Hashem says so; Hashem protects you;
Hashem can punish you." Hard in a world where people think
God asks them to defend their land unto death or civil war, to
bomb buses and buildings. Hashem, the colloquial term for
God whose very informality suggests a privileged relationship:
"I know what God wants of me."

I cannot appropriate God's name, but I will use it. I believe
in it. My practice exceeds a commitment to community, history, nationalism, nostalgia. So I use God's name with my
daughter; in discussion with her father too. I do not plan to
close discussion with variations on "Because God says so," but
I will rely upon the language of obligation, of task and necessary commitment.

Ori will have to answer her in his way. Maybe through the
songs he composes on his guitar, his lyrics in Hebrew and in
English both; or the classes in Midrash and Jewish philosophy
that he teaches adults and teenagers; or the projects designed
by the small, wonderful community of artists and activists
among whom he used to live in Brooklyn, whose ideas reach
us now in Michigan; or his work on the relation between the
Bible and seventeenth-century British poetry and politics.

When we tried to answer these questions in advance of
Priya, in advance of a wedding; when we tried to deal with

hypothetical, imagined points of conflict, we didn't get very far. We just got back to ourselves.

You cannot answer these questions without a whole life, and, if you can envision it to begin with, a whole life together. Ardent and earnest. A table with books spread upon it. A child wrapped in a tallis against a warm, swaying body.

A tallis over our heads as we drink the wine and the ring is slipped onto my finger. . . . .

In the first and second trimesters of Priya's development, before the pregnancy is visible and as it becomes visible, I teach two courses on Genesis, one to a group of college women and one to a group of Detroit Jews who gather weekly to study as adults; this group too is mostly women.

Genesis, I see suddenly, is a book all about the desire for children. Not even for children but for a single, precious child. The book of Exodus would be the story of full fertility, where mothers gave birth, as the Midrash has it, to six hundred thousand babies at once: fecundity without precedent in the face of terrible oppression. Yet Genesis was about the difficulty and extraordinary human desire for children, one child at a time, in a world not unusually inhospitable. Genesis was about the length of time it took before the idea of prayer seized our foremothers and fathers and they allowed God to answer and remember them with a new generation.

As I taught the book, I also listened to it chanted in the synagogue, week after week. I measured my own body's time against the time it took to read the narrative and the time the narrative recorded. My baby felt to me hundreds of years old as together we made our rapid way through those early generations, those miracle mothers and miracle births. Like old crones, it seemed the baby and I had seen it all, outlived them all: the young Sarah, then the old; the girl Rebecca all the way to the dying matriarch Rachel. The baby and I had the wisdom of eternity inside us.

At the same time, all the prolonged waiting of the fore-mothers: how mercifully it was abridged! In courses of seven days, we saw its historical relief. And the baby and I: we too were young again! Decades shrank back to days. Only a week had elapsed. And in this time against the backdrop of time, the baby grew.

When I taught Genesis, my audience was always one more than it seemed. No one knew about Priya. She was my secret, a secret whose contents I did not know, a secret only half believed in because it was so strange and impossible and wanted. My voice rose and fell in hours and hours of teaching, and in her office my doctor told me that by four months the fetus would recognize my timbre and my tone.

As I taught, I spoke to the classroom full of students, and I whispered to the child-to-be. The baby would know my voice not from ordinary speech alone but from the hours spent studying Torah together. A child knows the full Torah before it is born, the Sages teach. Only at the moment when the child leaves the womb does an angel tap it above the lip as a sign that all is now forgotten.

After hours of shared study, I thought, when my child left the womb, I would know some of what she had forgotten.

....

We live now in Ann Arbor, Michigan, the town in which I grew up. The synagogue we attend is not a formal congregation but a small university *minyan,* Orthodox in its orientation. Priya is one of very few babies at the *minyan,* in part because it is dominated by college students, but also because there is no *eruv* in Ann Arbor. An *eruv* is a legal device that tenders the status of a private area upon what we would consider a public area. According to Jewish law, one cannot carry on the Sabbath—and this includes carrying or strolling babies who cannot yet walk independently. As a Jewish legal term, "carrying" means not lifting an object and transporting it along with you but, more specifically, moving an object from one *r'shut,* one delineated area of ownership, to another. The *eruv,* made usually of preexisting telephone wires and connective tissue of one sort or another, allows Jews to carry because it makes of an extended area one space. It says, you are not crossing boundaries here; there are no boundaries within the *eruv.* Your town or neighborhood becomes your own backyard.

To set up an *eruv* and allow for pushing babies and toddlers in strollers, wheeling the elderly or disabled in wheelchairs, bringing a book or your tallis to shul, there are highly complex Jewish laws. How many people traverse this area? How far can a space extend and still be imagined as private? A rabbinic expert must be brought in to gauge the possibilities. A representative of the community must contact other Jewish groups in the town to ask for support. Another representative must first explain and then negotiate with the electric company for the use of its poles to set up the physical frame delineating the enclosed space. Then there is the matter of cost: paying for the rabbinic specialists, any city fees, electric company charges, materials. Finally, the *eruv* needs checking weekly before the Sabbath. If it is not checked and a part of the enclosure has fallen or become in some way not kosher, a whole community will be going about its business heedlessly sinning. The activities will be the same, but with an *eruv,* they are kosher. Without, they are a grave transgression. Innocence, sanction, is not personal or defined by action. Innocence is existential.

We are working now on setting up an *eruv* in Ann Arbor. All Orthodox Jews know that a community is not fully viable until it has one because it cannot attract observant young families, the families that procreate and keep a community thriving and growing. Here in Ann Arbor, a relatively small number of families—no more than twenty—care deeply about an *eruv.* Perhaps, one might think, it is not worth the enormous effort and expense for so few Jews. And yet for the mothers and the elderly and disabled, it is a matter of vital concern. Why do I say "mothers" and not "parents"? Only men are obligated to pray in a *minyan,* a public quorum. In a truly Orthodox household, if someone cannot go to shul, it is going to be the mother who stays home. For Ori and me, this is not a fundamental divide. Between the two of us, obligation should be equal. As a matter of self-understanding, obligation is actually mine.

Well before our child was born, I worried about this prohibition against carrying that meant the difference between a public life for an infant and parent on Shabbat or a life wholly indoors. When Priya was a tiny infant, I wore her in the sling and considered my "carrying" of her a form of wearing. She was inseparable from me. I wore the sling from the moment we walked out the door of our home until the moment we arrived back home. I did not see myself as carrying her. All the literature on sling wearing describes the parent as "wearing the child." This cultural understanding weighed with me too. My choice was not acceptable to most Orthodox Jews halakhically—that is, legally—but it was the compromise that made best sense to me. Mothers of young children who live without an *eruv,* yet abide by Jewish laws, do not leave the home on Shabbat—not for synagogue, not for socializing. I did not want to be a shut-in, especially in the early days of Priya's life, when seeing other people was more vital than eating.

But even more pressing, I wanted Priya in shul, in synagogue. I wanted it familiar as milk: the rhythms, the abiding and alternating demands for respect, silence, participation, directed vision; the particular sociality of it—you don't converse with your neighbor, but you acknowledge her; the mores of Kiddush, the communal gathering that follows the service, where you engage in small talk and small eating for fifteen minutes or so. I wanted it all known to her.

I think she and I have succeeded in creating this familiarity. Priya is what a friend of mine calls "a shul baby." A baby who not only does not mind shul, but in fact feels right at home, can live patiently in this demanding environment as if she were a well-trained adult or, alternatively, a child mesmerized by some visible thing. My friend's "shul baby" is now nineteen, and he often leads the services. He is tall, much taller than his mother, and yet she sees him still as the one of her three children who really took to shul. Priya takes to many things. I don't know yet if she has a special affinity for shul, and I don't know what she will be like in this environment as a toddler. What I can say is that right now she is very good at this thing.

But when I talk about this with my friend, when I see her eyes travel the length of the son who was once her baby, I begin to wonder, is there such a thing as a girl "shul baby"?

．．．．．．．．．．．．

My best friend from childhood gave birth to a girl a few years ago and named her Binah. She blessed her beautiful new daughter with the term that I had associated in the late 1980s and early 1990s with the severe limitations on women's learning. Binah, not *hokhmah*. Binah: an excuse for teaching women less than they needed to know.

But now it is 2005, 5765. A small, bright girl named Binah will begin school next year. Perhaps in twelve or thirteen years she will study in Israel among other young women; perhaps she will not be the only Binah. Perhaps the name will catch fire.

Today in Jerusalem female high school graduates no longer learn in kitchens or converted apartments. My days of "Binah" are over. I know this from the most material of evidence: tables, chairs, classrooms, libraries, Batei Midrash. Where once there was plastic and rusting metal, chairs impossible to sit in, folding tables liable to collapse at a breeze, desks with shaky, uneven legs, buckling bookshelves, now there is real, hard wood. Oak and maple chairs and tables. Built-in bookcases across long walls. Wide, strong surfaces on which to set your books, your pile of books, your entire future of learning.

A student of mine here at the University of Michigan tells me that last year when she was learning in Israel, it was the young men, not the women, who were frustrated. The boys wanted to learn Bible, not only Talmud. They were envious of the rich offerings of the girls' programs, of the care taken to devise these programs.

Today these girls-turning-into-women have much of what they need. They have full libraries, holy books with bookplates attesting not to the haphazard life of given-away books but to donations earmarked just for them. The institutions at which these girls learn are not upstarts, start-ups, anymore but have become the establishment itself.

If you live in Jerusalem or New York, you can see that the contours of Jewish life have changed radically in the last fifteen years. There is a Jewish Orthodox Feminist Alliance out of New York which has an annual conference that attracts hundreds of participants, women and some men as well. Also in New York there are Orthodox rabbinic intern programs that hire both male rabbis and female scholars as assistants to their senior rabbis. There are a few Modern Orthodox congregations where it is common to see young women in *talleisim,* in prayer shawls and head coverings that signify not only marriage, but also the sort of bowing one's head that male yarmulkes indicate.

Minyanim, prayer groups, pop up where the defining features are the elements of women's participation: women leading prayers that do not require a quorum, such as the Friday night service of Psalms, Kabbalat Shabbat; women reading from the Torah on their own side of the *mehitza;* women reading from the Torah for the whole congregation, yet not reciting the blessings over the Torah. Torah scrolls get carried through women's sections in prayer, get handed across the *mehitza,* and women give *divrei Torah,* discourses of Torah, as a matter of course. Today there are a few women presidents of Orthodox congregations, and more and more mainstream Orthodox synagogues advertise classes with women teachers and scholars-in-residence. New York and Jerusalem overflow with young and youngish women, in their mid-twenties through their mid-thirties, teaching, learning, praying, no longer discussing whether to cover their hair or wear pants (or discussing only briefly).

And then, beyond the pale of even liberal Orthodoxy, there is full-fledged egalitarianism. The shock of full-fledged egalitarianism is not that someone is doing it somewhere. In my lifetime there have always been egalitarian prayer settings for women. The shock of today's egalitarian prayer is *who* is doing it. It's the girls I grew up with. Not all of them of course. Many of the girls I grew up with pray in mainstream Orthodox synagogues in small communities and medium-sized cities. In these places the changes I mention are absent. Their effects are still few, though perhaps only unmeasurable as yet. And a significant percentage of the girls with whom I grew up—and the girls growing up now—pray in the transitional sort of worlds I have just described.

But then there are the women who were once "Brovender's girls," with me, in the late 1980s and early 1990s, in our long skirts and troubled minds, pants and dismayed bodies. A small but significant percentage of these women—I can think easily of twelve or fourteen—now pray in fully egalitarian communities. They read from the Torah before men; they lead men and women and children in prayer; they wear or do not wear *talleisim;* when they do, it is often with a hat; they sit beside men or beside women only, but they lead.

How to explain the sea change I am talking about? These women, now in the egalitarian *minyanim,* are learned Jews. They grew up fluent in Hebrew, fluent in Bible, some fluent in Talmud. They grew up in kosher homes, in Orthodox and occasionally Conservative day schools; they were told by male principals to cover their knees and elbows; they played basketball in skirts. They are the real thing, the real Modern Orthodox thing. They are not feminists turning to Orthodox Judaism in a kind of American backlash, and they are not Conservative

Jewish women reasonably insisting on a timely form of religion, and they are not Reform women who, also reasonably, have never considered what it would be like to sit behind a *mehitza*. They are post-Orthodox Jewish women who are not even post-Orthodox because they still learn and they still pray; their homes are strictly kosher; many of them teach (though often in universities rather than Jewish institutions); the careers they have developed come second to the dictates of Jewish law, and their children. . . .

Their children. Our children. It is a problem. Where will our children study? And how will our children get to shul in small towns without an *eruv*? And in those same towns, which are *not* Jerusalem or New York, how will we create communities of prayer where no girl must imagine herself falling from the balcony, twirling through the air toward a life that is imaginable no other way but as a sort of freefall that cannot end well?

....

Ori and Priya and I pray regularly, we "daven" in our Orthodox *minyan,* but we worry about the immediate future, which is really just the present: our own and hers. Non-Jewish friends of ours, and some Jewish friends, say, "What about the Conservative synagogue? Couldn't she lead there?" My hesitation to make that switch comes not only from my appreciation for the members of our small community, friends who have become like a second family to us in both ordinary times and times of need.

I have a history in Conservative Judaism. By the time I was a Bat-Mitzvah, I had prayed with my parents and siblings in three Conservative synagogues. We had lived walking distance from these congregations and walked to shul. Cars had pulled into the parking lots of the shul as we walked up its path alone. When a car door opened, you might hear music dying down from a radio or cassette deck as the engine quietly turned off. Women carried purses; men's wallets were visible in pockets.

In the morning before we left for shul my brother and sister and I were eager to watch cartoons on Saturday morning; no, it's Shabbat, my parents said. I missed writing on Shabbat. I also missed the birthday parties of children I knew from the neighborhood who celebrated on Saturdays. But it was Shabbat. A day of difference. This was why we walked; this was why no television, no writing, no money, no cars.

But at the Conservative synagogue few families lived this way. We were the odd ones out. I once heard a woman say to her husband about the five of us, sitting in a row with our prayer books, "They're *real* Jews." We did not wear black hats or long black coats, and yet we were the real Jews. We did not need to be told on which page we could find the prayers. Was my father a rabbi? another child wanted to know. He's a chemical engineer, I said. "Well," the kid said, "he looks like a rabbi because he's always on the stage." When I asked my father about it, he said, "Anyone who knows how to read from the Torah can be on the *bimah;* you don't have to be a rabbi at all." "So why aren't there lots of different people on the *bimah* each week?" I asked. People don't know Hebrew, my father said. They don't how how to read.

"They're Orthodox," my friend Danny's mother explained to him. But we weren't Orthodox. There we were in an egalitarian service, for starters. But in the Conservative synagogue in Midwestern America, somehow we *were* Orthodox. My parents' education in Hebrew and *yiddishkeit,* Jewishness, marked them as different. My parents' consistency with us, their children, marked them and us as "real Jews." In New York or Philadelphia or Boston or Los Angeles, cities with vibrant centers of Jewish study and rabbinic training, we would likely have found other Conservative Jews who observed and studied and made Judaism the prism for their choices, yet in Mid-America we were often alone.

Among our synagogue's members, some homes were kosher; some were not. Some people ate only kosher food in their homes but had McDonald's when they were out. Some parents stayed home from work and went to shul on the Jewish holidays that fell during the week; most did not. Some people went to shul every week but would make an exception for competing events here and there. Even few of the Shabbat regulars came to pray at weekday services unless they were saying the mourners' kaddish.

To me, at twelve, thirteen years old, it seemed a chaos of ways of being in the world. This was not because people were selecting ways in which to participate and ways in which to abstain; all Jews, all religious people make such choices. To me it seemed a chaos because the choices did not seem *difficult*. The conflict among alternatives was not acknowledged. Jews around me simply seemed to be living calmly in two separate worlds: the synagogue and the home, the home and outside the home, Shabbat and the week; Jewish and normal.

Conservative Judaism was not at its best in the synagogue world; it attracted many parents who wanted nothing more than a Bar- or Bat-Mitzvah for their kids, a respectable annual High Holidays destination. Its best was its day schools, the nationwide Solomon Schechter system, and its summer camps, the Ramah network. In these venues you could see true hope for the movement: a strong emphasis on bilingualism, which enabled a meaningful approach to Jewish rituals and texts. These were the places where you could find the impassioned leaders and families.

But by the time I was in eighth grade the juice had run out. In all Chicago and its suburbs, a major center of Jewish living in America, there was no Conservative Jewish high school. What could this mean? What good middle-class or aspiring American parent would let a child drop out of school after eighth grade? What good Jewish parent would tell a child that he or she knew all that was necessary for life by the age of thirteen?

My parents enrolled me in the sole coed Jewish high school in Chicago, an Orthodox school. A year later my family moved to the largely Orthodox suburb of Skokie. Here, in the enclosed world of American Modern Orthodoxy, Jewish *was* normal. Here no one went to McDonald's—not once, not ever. Here when you missed Saturday morning cartoons, no other kids had seen them either, so had you even really missed them? Here a weekday holiday brought as many people to shul as an ordinary Shabbat—no matter that you had to skip two days of work. There were the more religious and the less religious, certainly, but everyone walked to shul. The shul had no parking lot.

Soon enough the novelty of normalcy would cease to suffice. I would finish high school and travel to Israel to confirm what I had begun to guess: that homogeneity and lackluster performance and sidelined women were a disaster of their own. But I had, at the very least, found the movement to work against. And if in 1989 the chairs in the girls' Beit Midrash were plastic or rusting metal, if the books were scared up from lost and disbanded institutions, if the House of Study was a barely converted kitchen, and if I had never open a volume of the Talmud until I was almost twenty, at least by joining up with the Orthodox, I had gained five years more of study at a time where there was nowhere else those lessons could be had.

At least there *was* a Beit Midrash.

Now, twenty years later, its doors are usually open. Sometimes the wood gleams. ....

A few weeks ago I took my English students for a tour of the university library; an excellent librarian led us through. I like to do this with first-year students because many of them find Google sufficient for their research, and the library shelves are too often left undisturbed. Then too university libraries can intimidate the uninitiated.

It would be nearly impossible for me to convey to my students what the university library meant to me when I was a college student. For starters, I was astounded and moved that there were weeks at a time, at the end of each semester, that it never closed. Its doors simply never closed; they never locked against students or the night. In those years when I was looking for open libraries—looking for what the Victorians called "sympathy" or "fellow-feeling"—my ability to enter the library at any time of day or night granted it a sanctity that no other university building could have possessed.

I know that the history of women in the American academy has been and remains troubled and that Jews too once found doors closed against them in these universities. But by the 1990s the American university offered an Orthodox Jewish woman something she could not get anywhere else: knowledge, the capacity to teach it at the highest levels, and a degree that did not differentiate on the basis of sex. When I got married, I received a card from a friend of many years, a friend with whom I had gone to high school who now also teaches in a university. Its address read, "Mr. and Mrs. Ori Weisberg, in care of Dr. Ilana Blumberg." It is nice to be a Jewish woman with a degree of her own.

It is not surprising that I have chosen, for the time being at least, to make my professional home in the world of the university. This personal choice seems not merely idiosyncratic to me when I recognize how many of my close female friends have entered academia and how many in Judaic Studies. We teach Bible, Midrash, and Talmud; Jewish literature in Yiddish, Hebrew, English, and European languages; Jewish history and religion; comparative religion and anthropology. We have written dissertations and now books on the translation of the sermon into a women's form of Hebrew literature, on the Midrashic responses to women's birthing bodies, on the laws of menstrual purity, on a major female Hebrew modernist writer, on Victorian women and the ethic of self-sacrifice, and also on subjects less notably involved with being women.

Would some of these female scholars have become rabbis had Orthodox Judaism allowed it? It seems likely. But in the absence of that choice, it is far easier to be a wife and mother and scholar in the university, difficult as that is, than to live full-time in the Orthodox Jewish world where one is always a woman before anything else.

My own teaching is mainly not in Judaic Studies, though it seems that with each year, I move a bit closer to half and half. I chose English Literature precisely because it was not home. Loving it as I did, I knew also its foreignness. Making English my "field" meant leaving the shtetl, living in a world in which no one would know my parents or grandparents or my kindergarten teacher who had seen such promise in me. I would be free to say and write what I wanted (I would have to find something to say and write), and I would also have to prove myself. No family. No one understanding things before I explained them. No shortcuts. I would be an adult, not the end of a long line of generations that brought my infant or girlhood self to the table each time an older scholar spoke to me.

English meant the challenge of figuring out what all those terms about church meant: vicars, parsons, surplices, parishes, synods, saints' days. Figuring out the important differences between Protestants and Catholics: all not Jewish. It meant attending functions where ham was served and the wine was not kosher and the dresses were low cut. It was glamour and adulthood and something from which I could walk away easily at the end of the day. Something I could say no to. Something to which I would have to say no.

Yes and no seem less clear to me now. Family seems less clear. My daughter and the son of my non-Jewish colleague play together regularly. She and I were pregnant at the same time; the children are close in age. The lines between houses, the lines between studies: they blur.

Love seems more clear, more recognizable than ever before. Repetition is not only a compulsion but a function of love, one of my professors once said in a discussion of Freud. I reread the same books over and over, in two languages. I have found and I find love in two languages. And actually in many more. Words are only a small part of things.

. . . .

We named Priya in shul on the last day of Passover, in the Jewish year 5764. Ori named her. I was at home, still recovering. Priya was at home, still learning to eat and sleep in a world outside the womb.

When Ori came home, the child had a name. Priya Rivka. Named for two of Ori's grandparents—his maternal grandfather, Ephraim, and his paternal grandmother, Hasia Rivka. We invented the name Priya, though I learned this past winter in Jerusalem that there is another Priya for ours to meet one day; she is now Bat-Mitzvah. Our Priya had no name until after her birth. We did not know her sex; we had a list of possible names for both sexes, and I had no inclination toward any of them. Until I saw a child, saw a real, live body that could breathe on its own, I could not consider names seriously.

When our baby was born, on the fourth day of Passover, all the girl names we had listed faded away. We could not even remember where we had put the list. Her face was like a little fruit, and Ori said, "What do you think of Priya? We could call her Pri."

Pri means fruit in Hebrew. On Passover we read the Song of Songs in synagogue. *Yavo dodi l'gano v'yochal pri m'gadav,* יבוא דודי לגנו ויאכל פרי מגדיו: "Let my beloved come to his garden and eat of his delicious fruit." ופריו מתוק לחכי: "And his fruit," the other replies, "was sweet to my palate." The ancient rabbis interpret these verses to refer to the history of God and Israel: how sweet the Torah was to the palate of Israel, how beloved the fruit of Israel was to God. Priya, fruit of God: the Torah is hers; the people of Israel are hers. Her life is bound up in both.

Her face is like a little fruit. And her middle name is Rivka, Hebrew for Rebecca. I have always found it complicated that we name our children for biblical characters. So early on we learn that these characters are human, flawed, troubled by circumstances beyond their control, even as they are also blessed, remembered, and honored in memory. How should we choose which troubles we want to evoke against the faces of our newborn children?

These days I set aside Rebecca's story, preferring the name Priya, which has no story attached, just images and associations. But I cannot escape the most striking verse about Rebecca: *va'tipol me'al ha'gamal,* ותפל מעל הגמל. Genesis 24, verse 64: astride her camel, Rebecca saw from afar the man who was to become her husband. According to graceful translations, she alighted from her camel and bowed low, then covered herself with her scarf in modesty, perhaps in the desire to retain a vital privacy.

According to my first, intensely literal translation, the translation of an eight-year-old learning on her own, Rebecca saw Jacob coming and did not dismount, controlled and calm, but instead *va'tipol:* she fell right off her camel, the way a child learning to walk might fall, just topple over; the way you fall when extraordinarily surprised or overcome, tripped up by life.

If our Priya fell off a camel, it would be as a comic act: to delight herself, to delight those who watch her. Humor, a quality often missing in biblical accounts, is a strong suit of hers. As open as an apple, she is a child full of joy and expression. Her eyes crinkle when she laughs, and her cheeks are like round berries. For Purim last month she was a perfect strawberry.

What is hidden in Priya, behind the scarf, is her future.

Acknowledgments

I would like to thank the Barnard College Centennial Scholarship Program under whose auspices this project began. This book bears the traces of my many outstanding professors at Barnard College, as well as the gifted teachers who prepared me for that relatively late phase of my education.

I thank Ladette Randolph at the University of Nebraska Press for her commitment to this book and her work on its behalf.

I would like to acknowledge the National Council of Jewish Women, in whose *Jewish Women's Literary Annual* excerpts from "Binah" were first published. The *Michigan Quarterly Review* and *Image: A Journal of Religion and the Arts* graciously granted permission to reprint selections here. The Money for Women / Barbara Deming Memorial Fund provided valuable support at an early stage of writing.

For sparing the time to read "Binah" and respond thoughtfully though we had never met in person, I thank three inspiring Jewish women of letters: Ellen Frankel, Cynthia Ozick, and Ellen Umansky.

Many friends, family members, and colleagues read this work along its way to publication. In New York, Michelle Friedman Belfer, Susan Shapiro, Shana Sippy, and Jay Zachter encouraged me at a very early point with intelligence and warmth. Arthur Samuelson of Schocken Books suggested that the manuscript had a future long before I could see it and gave me my first free books from a publishing house. And Rob McQuilkin generously shared with me his editorial expertise.

In Israel, Ann K. Blumberg (z"l) read with the most personal of interests and a teacherly eye; I wish she could have lived to see the final product. Judy Hurwich (z"l) envisioned my first publication long before I could and materialized the hope by literally clearing a space for me on her bookshelves. Ziva Kosofsky's response to my prose in Hebrew built a precious link between my worlds. Avivah Zornberg's teaching has, for the last eighteen years, made deep my well of metaphors.

In Philadelphia, Peter Stallybrass gave me the extraordinary teacher's gift of a new category by which to think; his ideas and passions helped me name intuitions of my own. David Sachs read with his typical curiosity for all things human and responded with typical, yet astounding, wisdom. John Heon, logopunk extraordinaire, made an old manuscript seem new enough to require further editing, and at precisely the right moment. John Parker gave me *Dubliners* and much else. Erin O'Connor enthusiastically considered my work in the context of nineteenth-century novels. Houston Baker read not one but two drafts and responded with an honesty that is as hard to come by as it is valuable.

In Michigan, Rick Hilles prompted me to return to writing with his gentle, comical, and sympathetic understanding of working against serious odds. Yofi Tirosh incorporated my work into her own and so doubled its value. In cyberspace, Linda Dowling supported and celebrated my scholarly and literary efforts, no matter their outcome. Tresa Grauer transformed this manuscript with her graceful, generous, and generative reading; with our daughters racing about underfoot, she encouraged me to tell a wider story than my own. Ori Weisberg made the hardest writing at the very end easy as Sunday morning coffee and our favorite baked goods.

I thank Sheila Jelen, אחות נוף מולדתי, not only for her careful reading of the manuscript at both initial and final stages, but also for the great honor she did me by sharing my work with her students. I owe this book's title in part to her trustworthy ear (and her ready laugh).

I thank Mary Gordon for her faith. Her mentorship and friendship continue to coax the best from me.

To my friends Ariela Freedman, Jeremy Wexler, Diane Halivni, Devorah Lissek, Josh Barash, Tammy Jacobowitz, Ronnie Perelis, Talya Kalender, Rebecca Kobrin, Sarah Levine, Helise Lieberman, Shifra Malina, Alison Morantz, Nomi Porten, Shulie Rubin, Joanna Samuels, Miryam Segal, and Amy Stern Gottesfeld, my appreciation for their copious gifts over many years.

To the Redlich family, *todah rabah* for allowing me to feel I always had a home in Israel. To the Weisbergs, Marilyn, Sidney (z"l), Ruth, and Aviva, and to Leah Blumberg, my gratitude for their loving support of my pursuits.

That my siblings appear rarely in these pages means only that their privacy is important to me; they occupy the most important place in my life, and I cannot envision my childhood or my life today without them beside me. To Jonathan and Rayli Blumberg, my gratitude for the way they always put family first; their steadfast love goes a very long way. Dear Jessica Abby, Emily Arielle, and William Evan have given me total delight from the moment I met each one of them; I wish for them all the blessings of childhood and all the blossomings of adulthood. Naomi Blumberg has given me the gifts of a friendship that is sturdier than any other.

To Ori and Priya, my beloved little family, נשיקות וחיבוקים וחיוכים, *n'shikot v'hibukim v'hiukhim:* kisses and hugs and bright smiles. Nothing more abstract will suffice.